Sam's Story

Sam's Story

South Dakota Through WWII Europe

Sam A. and Stella Nusz

iUniverse, Inc.
Bloomington

Sam's Story
South Dakota Through WWII Europe

iUniverse books may be ordered through booksellers or by contacting:

iUniverse
1663 Liberty Drive
Bloomington, IN 47403
www.iuniverse.com
1-800-Authors (1-800-288-4677)

ISBN: 978-1-4759-2253-0 (sc)
ISBN: 978-1-4759-2254-7 (hc)
ISBN: 978-1-4759-2255-4 (ebk)

Printed in the United States of America

iUniverse rev. date: 05/17/2012

Sam's Story:
South Dakota Through WWII Europe

Table of Contents

Sam's Story

Sam's Story

Sam's Story

Sam's Story

Preface

Sam A. Nusz, Dad, has a lifelong commitment to our country
behind his Midwest farmer/mechanic facade.   Like so many of the
WWII veterans he fought hard, endured much pain, lost buddies
but kept going to keep America safe. These veterans saw first-
hand the effects poor government leadership inflicts on people.
Americans have been fortunate in that we have not contended with
this brutality. These strong WWII Veterans fought hard, now it is
our turn to fight for America keeping a safe place for our families
to live. Dad's prayer is the United States can remain a stable
government; a safe home for future generations and we will never
experience the ravages of war.

Dad kept his experiences to himself until the 50th Anniversary of
the Normandy invasion. It was at that time he felt comfortable
sharing some moments from the war. Mom, Stella Nusz, and Dad
understand the value of history so proceeded to document some of
Dad's experiences and events of his military tour. Mom and Dad
initially documented these experiences for our family but felt a
need to share them with those interested in learning about the
ravages of WWII.

The short stories compiled in this book represent many hours of
Dad telling and retelling his experiences and Mom writing and re-
writing in order to accurately document events of Dad's life. These
short stories have been written over a twenty year time. Very little
editing was done to ensure their spirit and sentiments could be

shared with each reader. All the pictures were taken by Dad or his buddies.

Sam's Story:
South Dakota Through WWII Europe

Experienced and related by Sam A. Nusz
Compiled by Stel Nusz

1942

For our children: Philip, Jeffrey, and Norma

Sam's Story

Transcribed by Granddaughter, Nicole Nusz Kruse
until Stel, after a fashion learned to use the computer.

Edited by Norma Nusz Chandler

Cover designed by Jill Nusz Mettler

CHILDHOOD MEMORIES

MY LITTLE RED BASEBALL CAP

October 1924, the year the Meridian Bridge was dedicated was also the month and year I turned five year of age.

The day of the Meridian Bridge dedication at our house, started with much excitement and anticipation as our father was making arrangements with an uncle to go to Yankton, to join in the celebration.

At the appointed time of departure Dad, Mom, my brother, two sisters, Uncle Bill, Aunt Lizzie, cousin Ray Herrboldt, and myself, wearing my little red baseball cap, boarded our black touring car. I got to sit at the right hand corner on the back seat.

As we were traveling up the steep hill by the Jim River, a gust of wind caught my little red baseball cap and lifted it off my head. While I was watching it sail off into the ditch, I hollered and hollered and hollered but to no avail, the grinding of the car motor and the adults, thoroughly engrossed in conversation, drown out my plea.

After the dedication of the Meridian Bridge, we drove across to Nebraska on the new bridge, as that day the people could cross without paying toll.

Eventually we left for home. When we came to the approximate place where my little red baseball cap took flight, Dad stopped and we went searching, but to no avail. We did not find it. I was heavy hearted over this situation for a long time but eventually I consoled myself thinking, some other little fellow must have become the owner of my little red baseball cap, of which I was so fond and proud.

For me, the day of the Meridian Bridge dedication didn't end as happily as it had begun.

At times when I think of the events of Meridian Bridge Day, I get kinda nostalgic about my little red baseball cap.

Sam's Story

A MEMORABLE   RABBIT HUNT

In our younger years, my brother Andy, Rueben Jensen, a good friend who lived a half mile down the road from our farm and myself would take our '28 Chevy car and go jack rabbit hunting. This was an evening activity during winter months. At that time gas was 08 to 15 cents a gallon.

During that era, 'The Depression Years' (some of the 1930s), we earned spending money selling rabbit, weasels and skunk pelts. Badgers, fox and coyote pelts could also be sold, if you were fortunate enough to trap or hunt them down, so to say. At that time there wasn't a fur buyer in Menno. We received flyers in the mail from the Twin Cities and Chicago, stating the price for the pelts. The flyer also included instructions as to how we were to pack and send the pelts.

Rabbit pelts brought 35 cents. Skunks were priced as to the width of the white stripe along the back of the skunk. The narrower the white stripe, the better the prices of the skunk pelt, also the larger the pelt the better the price. The skunk pelt could vary from five to twelve dollars.

As for weasel pelts, that was a bit tricky. If it was a 'brownish' one and was considered too immature, it was discarded.   However if it was a white mature one, it brought equal the price of a good skunk pelt. Pelts were purchased during winter months only.

Sam's Story

Well, this one winter evening, Rueben came over to show us his brand new, 22-repeater rifle. Andy and I had a 410 shotgun. We were enthused and enthralled about that repeater rifle. After examining and admiring it, we went hunting.

We took off for the pasture. I did the driving while Ruben and Andy each sat on the front fenders. Rabbits, being in the bright light of a car, become momentarily stunned and blinded. Soon we spotted a rabbit. It was sitting a ways off. I stopped the car. Naturally Rueben had first chance to try out his gun. Rueben aimed and fired four times, missing the rabbit every time. However, on the fifth try, when he aimed and fired---suddenly the rabbit took off---but the tail stayed lying on the ground.

After that event, Rueben was considered the best marksman. He could shoot the tail off a rabbit. HA, Ha, ha!!!

DEVELOPING A NEW MODEL

It was the year of 1938 that Dad, (your grandfather, F. August) became manager of the MENNO MERCANTILE (aka MENNO MERC, and /or THE MERC), a farm implement business in Menno, South Dakota. At that time MENNO MERC was a dealer for McCORMICK- DEERING tractor and equipment.

Late that summer some dealers from North Dakota and South Dakota received an invitation from McCORMICK- DEERING COMPANY to gather at Aberdeen, South Dakota, on a given date to have a "meeting of the minds", pertaining to a new model tractor.

The day of this occasion was a beautiful early fall day. Dad and I drove to Aberdeen. Arriving there, we found the location to be out in a huge, wide-open field! A sign stating: "PROVING GROUNDS", indicated to us, we were at the right place.

A short meeting was held in a portable workshop, the only building on the grounds. We were instructed and informed as to our involvement, pertaining to' a new model Farmall tractor'. Following the meeting, we went to the field where we were shown six tractors, available for us to use on this project. Some were painted black. The others were the raw metal. The tractors appeared identical but some had more horsepower than others. Plows, discs, duck foot, field cultivator and other farm implements were supplied for us to use with these tractors, and while using these implements with these tractors, we were to be alert to any change we might suggest to improve the efficiency and comfort of the tractor.

After a trial run, if we felt we had a viable idea, we returned to the workshop. If the suggestion was feasible to change at that time, "the engineers" made the change and again we were sent to the "proving grounds' for testing the changes.

Other ideas or suggestions were recorded on paper for future consideration at the factory.

As the activities of the day were winding down and dealers were reviewing the events of the day, ever so often the topic as to the color of the 'new model' surfaced. Talk, such as, "Do you suppose it will be green, yellow or black or gray?" was heard occasionally, while we were making 'small talk'.

When we arrived home, Dad and I summed the events of the day, as a challenging and stimulating experience.

Months later (1939), when the new model tractors were developed, using some of the improvements and suggestions of that day, the two models were "FARMALL H" and "FARMALL M". When the FARMALL-H arrived at THE MERC, it was painted the beautiful color, red. The FARMALL-M was also painted red.

Sam's Story

Up to this time, to start a tractor, it had to be cranked by hand. With the new models, FARMALL- H and FARMALL- M, people had the option to purchase a tractor with an electric starter or with a hand crank; the hand crank being cheaper. Also during this era the H and M FARMALL's were the only tractors in the United states the engine clutch could be changed without splitting the tractor to repair.

We purchased the first new model "H" that was shipped to MENNO MERC. This one did not have an electric starter on it. We needed to crank it. However, that winter, brother, Andy and myself equipped this tractor with a battery, a generator, a starter and lights from on old car. We now had a "push button start" tractor.

Eventually McCORMICK-DEERING became INTERNATIONAL HARVESTER. Today the company is known as CASE IH.

All in all, I found this to be an educational and interesting experience, and I am grateful I had the opportunity to be a part of such a project.

Sam's Story

MILKING MACHINE

Back in 1939 F. August Nusz became manager of Menno Mercantile (aka) 'The Merc'. The year of 1953, the F. August Nusz family became the owner of Menno Mercantile. Among employees, Harley Bittner was employed during the late 1940s and early 1950s.

By this time Rural Electrification Association (REA) had swept over many areas of the United States; Eastern South Dakota, being one of these areas which had received REA power at the time.

Because of REA many farmers, who were milking cows became excited about having a milking machine installed. The Merc had the agency for selling milkers. When F. August made a sale of a milker, he kindly added, the installers would do the first milking.

First thing was to place the vacuum pump in the separator room, wiring it for electric power. We then installed the pipe from one end of the cow stanchion to the end of the stanchion. Between every two cows a valve was placed to connect the milk bucket to the cow's milk bag, namely the four teats. This was often a challenge, as these four hoses which were attached to the cow's teats, also had a suction to squeeze the teat.

If, where we were installing a machine, this farmer had cats, dogs, and children running around behind the cows, the cows were quite complacent. However, where the cows were accustomed to only one individual who took care of the cows, it was a different story. Attaching the bucket to the cow, and the cow hearing the whish, whish of the hoses or any other unusual activity or strange noise, disturbed her to the point of Harley ending in the gutter and Sam rescuing him. Milking all those cows that evening has been a memorable event. Ever so often visiting with Harley's, this incident surfaced. However, now it was considered humorous.

Note: This was said about REA back in 1935, when REA came about. "REA is the second best thing that ever happened, the best thing that ever happened was the Love of God."

MENNO BAKERY

Back in 1953 Joe and Yvonne Espedal of Mitchell, South Dakota purchased the bakery in Menno. Mr. Espedal brought his own electric powerized equipment, however there was a problem. His equipment was all wired for 220 volt and the building was wired for 110 volt only. He then hired Sam to rewire all the electric power driven equipment.

GUESS DOC GLANZER'S BILL

Remember this era Dad is telling about was before modern technology, like tractors, before rubber tires on tractors, combines and modern farm equipment. Most of farming at that time was done with workhorses Dad, (F. Aug.) had eight workhorses. Your great grandfather Nusz had twenty-eight workhorses).

During the fall of 1937, at different times bronco horses were herded from the western part of the state, to various sale barns, in this part of the state, to sell. A bronco is a western U.S., small wild, unbroken horse.

George Martin, (who at the time lived about two and one half miles south of Jeff's farm, where Jonas's live), was one of about four or five young fellows who rode out west to round up these broncos and herd them to the Menno Sale Barn.

Dad (F.August) would on occasion buy one or two, two year or three year old broncos for five, ten or fifteen dollars apiece. When broken, they were used for riding or hitching to a buggy.

The broncos that weren't sold were herded out to, what was once a farm across the US-81, from the Jonas farm. Presently there is one small building remaining and every summer someone places beehives on this property.

Sam's Story

At that time a family by name of Karonda lived there. The father dug board wells. I went to school with some of the Karonda children at Molan District #60. The broncos were kept in Karonda's pasture until they were taken to a glue factory, we were told.

Now, before brother Andy and myself would break a bronco, they were halter trained. They mingled with our workhorses out in the pasture and would enter the barn to be fed.

One day I had time and decided to take the shiny, all black beauty, bronco out to start breaking her. After having put the saddle on her, I led her out back of the barn, toward the pasture. I got on her back to try to ride her. She bucked a bit and threw herself backwards on her back. Up righting herself, I jumped on her back again. She reared up and again fell on her back. I thought this occurred due to slightly muddy conditions and decided to wait until the ground would be in more favorable condition.   .

Therefore one day when the conditions seemed OK and I wasn't especially busy, I again put the saddle on her, led her out behind the barn, got on her back and immediately tried to make her run. I succeeded for about 100 yards, when she stopped on all fours, and threw herself backwards again. Being I lost my balance, she fell on me.

Sam's Story

The next thing I remember, Andy had come with the car where I was lying. He helped me into the car and drove to the house, where Mom and Andy put me on the couch. It was very painful.

Dr. Glanzer was called. When he arrived, I was placed on a chair while Doc examined me. The diagnosis was: my back was broken in two places and my pelvis was also broken. Also, I was badly bruised where the saddle horn jabbed me and slide off below my ribs on my left side.

What did Doc do? Doc wrapped me up like a mummy; with adhesive tape that I thought was 10 inches wide, (I doubt that it was that wide, more like 6 inches wide, maybe) from under my arms to below my hips. (Adhesive tape of that time is hard to describe. It was composed of some sturdy, white material, covered with some powerful sticky stuff. It was painful to remove).

I can't remember taking pain pills. Pain medication, during that era wasn't as prevalent and available as it is today. I do remember the terrible pain!!

I remember not really sleeping for; I think three days and three nights. I remember groaning. Then one evening Uncle Emil Saylers came to visit. Uncle Emil sat by my bedside and recognizing my misery, handed me a cigarette and said, "Here Sam, smoke a cigarette."

Not having smoked, to speak of, at that time in my life, I vigorously inhaled. That cigarette put me to sleep and the next thing I knew, it was the next day. And I felt some better.

Looking around, I noticed Uncle Emil had left a pack of cigarettes by my bedside. So there is something good to be said about cigarettes.

After some time, the adhesive from the tape was starting to loosen to the point; Mom could start releasing a portion of it every day, until I as free of that powerful adhesive tape. I started using crutches after about three months. I then graduated to the use of a cane. I used the cane as little as possible. Finally I was able to walk without support!

And guess what Doctor Andrew Glanzer charged for this episode in my life!!! He charged TWO DOLLARS!!

It seems it wasn't too long after that episode that Uncle Sam drafted me into the service on March 22, 1941. Then Uncle Sam really taught me how to walk, eventually walking twenty-six miles in six hours.

FEBRUARY 1941 --- MARCH 1944

TRAINING, BEFORE GOING OVERSEAS

It was an ordinary winter day, early in the year of 1941 when in our mail there was a letter for me. From the return address I felt sure I knew what the message would be. The letter contained my draft card—number 123.

From then on the focus of my future had the underlying thought about being drafted.
Shortly thereafter I received a letter again with the same return. This time I was notified to report to Parkston, South Dakota, on a certain date for a physical examination.

After a short interval, I received another letter, with the now familiar return, informing me I was drafted and to report to Tripp, South Dakota, on March 22nd.

March 22nd soon arrived. Dad, (F. August,) took me to Tripp, SD. When all twenty-eight draftees assembled, we said our "Good Byes" and boarded a bus for Sioux Falls, South Dakota. We were the first draftees from Hutchinson County. Up to this time, there had been enough volunteers to fill the quota.

After arriving in Sioux Falls, we were again given a physical examination and passing the physical; we were inducted (sworn) into the United States Army for one year.
Following this process, we proceeded to the train depot and boarded the train, heading for Ft. Snelling, Minnesota. This was my first train ride. Here at Ft. Snelling we were issued an army uniform.

Figure 1: Sam sitting on his Mom and Dad's (Martha and F. August) front porch.

Sam's Story

The following day we again boarded a train. We left Ft. Snelling
and the train wended it's way into North Dakota, Montana, Idaho,
Washington, Oregon, and on down, more or less along the west
coast of California, to Camp Roberts, near San Miguel. We hadn't
gotten off the train since we'd left Ft. Snelling.

From the time we left Tripp, Ewald Aisenbrey of Menno was the
only person I knew. Here at camp we were assigned to different
units and thereafter rarely got to see one another.

Here we were fitted with a backpack. And basic training began.
For thirteen weeks we trained in the Infantry Division. We were
now given a furlough. (Remembering back to basic training, it
was a good thing).

During training I'd become acquainted with GIs from throughout
the USA. When we found out about the furlough, we were having
a conversation about traveling home and back. The one GI from
Chicago mentioned, when he returns after the furlough, he would
be driving back with his car. We then arranged that I would meet
him at an appointed place in Nebraska and I'd ride back to camp
with him from there. I can't remember how I got to Sioux Falls,
but from Sioux Falls, I took the bus to Menno. At that time there
was a bus route from Springfield, South Dakota to Sioux Falls and
back to Springfield the same day.

After the furlough we met. The GI who owned the car asked me to
drive. He climbed into the back seat of the car. Another GI was

with him but he didn't know about driving. It was a hard surfaced road, but the roads weren't engineered as well as now days. Driving in the mountains proved to be a challenge. The roads were narrow at that time in history, the curves were shorter, and tires weren't what they are now days. Tires then seemed to squeal on every curve. This was a new experience for me, as I'd only driven on back, country and gravel roads, on the prairies of South Dakota. This was before the main roads in our county were hard surfaced. And remember back then vehicles didn't go as fast as those of your era.

En route to California, we stopped at Las Vegas, Nevada. At that time 'Vegas' was quite a small town. It being breakfast time, we went looking for an eating-place. We couldn't find any. Believe it or not, we inquired from a person on the street. He pointed and told us, "Go down the street to the house with a few steps to the porch. They feed people". (Can you imagine Las Vega being so quaint?) Following his directions, we came to the house, walked up the steps and entered the house. We seated ourselves and the waitress came and took our order. When the food arrived, we enjoyed a substantial breakfast, paid up and went on our way.

Again the owner of the car asked me to drive. And again he got into the back seat. By the time we arrived at Camp Roberts, I was tired. If I ever knew why this GI didn't want to drive, I can't remember. (This was before South Dakota drivers had to have a driver's license.)

*Tent we slept in. A big
fort with ca......

Figure 2: Sam relaxing at Ft. Ord. A box tent can be seen in the background.

From Camp Roberts our unit was transferred to Camp Orb, in the San Luis Obispo, California, area. At this camp our unit was attached to the Anti-Tank Unit. While we were stationed here, three of us GIs were offered training for flying the P-38 planes. This offer included signing up for three extra years. At that time, those of us who were inducted were inducted for one year.

At that time Gran'pa (F. August) was owner and also managed MENNO MERCANTILE, aka MENNO MERC and/or THE MERC. This was before REA. At that time MENNO MERC had the WINCHARGER agency. It was at this time that the Wincharger was coming into its own. When Gran'pa made a sale, I'd set up the wind charger and wired the buildings for the farmer. Those farmers, who now had a Wincharger, if they wanted, could now have a milk machine installed. I also installed these machines. At times Harley Bittner also helped. (Another story for another time).

Then too I took care of the country telephone lines whenever there was a problem of sorts. At that time there were no wires underground. The electric or power and telephone wires were on poles, in the cities, towns and country. During the evenings I repaired battery, operated radios for people in the community, in the basement of our house. Gran'pa thought he had enough work to keep me busy at home. Therefore I declined the offer. The other two accepted.

Anyway, at Camp Ord we studied Anti-Tank guns, rifles, machine guns and Morse code. (Now that I'm redoing this story, February, 2006, this week this information was given on the news, "Samuel Morse invented the Morse Code in 1844. The first telegram was sent from Washington DC to Baltimore, Maryland. It stated, 'What God Hath Wrought.' This year ends the era of the telegram, as the last telegram has been sent. This came about because of the efficiency of the telephone, Internet, and email.) Also, we were taken to a desert, a place called "HUNDRED LEGGED". Here we trained to maneuver on sandy conditions!!! Driving in the desert was different than driving on regular roads or terrain. We learned very quickly that you couldn't do a quick take-off. If you did, immediately the drive wheels would sink into the sand and YOU WERE STUCK!!!

Figure 3: Sam standing by their sleeping quarters (box tent) at Ft. Ord.

Figure 4: Sam with Camp Ord in the background.

Sam's Story

Also while training at Camp Ord, this one-day a fire broke out in the mountains. About four-o'clock that afternoon several army trucks took about 150 of us GIs out to fight the fire. This was in an uninhabited area. The growth on this land was 'shrubbery', some trees and the area was completely covered with ripe, wild oats. The equipment we used to fight the fire was shovels and burlap bags. After we arrived at the fire, we were instructed about 'controlling the fire.' We were then told, "When you have finished fighting the fire, you remain in the area until the army trucks come again to pick you up. Do not start a fire to keep warm! Thus the fire observers will know the fire has been put out." After about four hours of fighting the fire, we had it controlled. So we waited and waited and waited some more---until the following forenoon before the army trucks came to pick us up. Until that time, this was the coldest night I'd ever spent in my life.

One day a Command car arrived at Hundred Legged. Charles Wilbur, a fellow GI, and myself were ordered to report to the Command car. We reported and were ordered to return to Camp Orb in the Command car. Arriving back at camp, Wilbur and I were placed with the heavy Field Artillery Unit. This unit was ready to take off for San Francisco, California.

When we arrived at San Francisco, we were taken to the dock where we boarded a ship. The ship soon left the harbor. Our destination was 'PLUM' or 'PLUMB', which was a code term for, "DESTINATION UNKNOWN." As I remember, we were sailing a day or so, when the ship made 'about face,' and we returned to the harbor. We were informed, "DESTINATION NO MORE." We were then told we had been on our way to Hawaii on December 7th, (1941), that fateful day in history, and we were no longer needed for that assignment. Now being war had been declared, all GIs were automatically in the service for the duration.

This turn of events caused an unexpected situation. Being there was no place to house us as yet, we were instructed to dismount and stay by the shore of the Golden Gate Bridge until further orders will be given. And the final command was, "DO NOT LEAVE THIS AREA"!! We were to remain here until a plan for us had been worked out. So we meandered around the area. I remember sleeping under the Golden Gate Bridge that night. While at this temporary location we were told the Japanese had fired shells at different places along the West Coast, planning to invade the United States. But somehow the Japanese presumed every family in the State had a gun or two in their possession. That thought was enough for them to scrap their idea. It was then they invaded the South Pacific Islands.

The following day we were moved to a shelter. The shelter was a huge warehouse. We were shown, on the cement floor, where we would bed down, using the two army blankets from our field pack. Finally, we were fed. We were a large troop of GIs and the echelons were finding things for us to do. The group I was with was sent to Los Angeles to guard the DOUGLAS AIRCRAFT PLANT.

Figure 5: Guarding at Hollywood.

While we were guarding there, the workers at the plant were building the largest aircraft of that day. It was called the "B-19". When it was completed, it was brought out to the runway for testing. This plane was so heavy, that on take-off, the cement runway crackled like when walking on thin ice. We were told the plane was flown to some place in Texas---not to be returned, but that it was disassembled in Texas.

While on this guard duty, we were stationed at Long Beach, where we lived in cabins. These cabins were a mile from the Douglas

Aircraft Plant. Army trucks shuttled us to our duty. This was sheer luxury. From there we were sent to North Hollywood Park, Los Angeles, we were given orders: "DO NOT LEAVE THESE PREMISES." We roved the park whenever we felt like it. While we camped here, we slept in pup tents. This was a relaxing two weeks. Even today, when I see the" HOLLYWOOD" sign on TV, I have good memories of that time, doing my army stint.

Figure 6: Camping in pup tents at Hollywood Park.

Sam's Story

I do not recall how long we guarded the Douglas Aircraft Plant. After our reprieve we received orders to move. We moved a ways north to San Miguel. Here we guarded an airport. Again, I can't remember how long we were on this assignment, when again we were on the move to the San Diego area. Here our camp was in the mountains. The assignment was to guard the SAN DIEGO WATER SUPPLY, in case of sabotage. It was a three-mile walk to our guard position. Our schedule when guarding was, four hours on, four hours off or eight hours on, eight hours off. San Diego had the best weather conditions I've ever experienced. The temperature was consistently nice while we were stationed here. We were told we would be receiving a furlough in the near future. Being our pay was twenty-one dollars a month but ten dollars was taken out for Life Insurance, plus two dollars for dry cleaning, we were looking for the cheapest kind of transportation. When we were given the date of the furlough, there were enough of us going east, to charter a bus to Salt Lake City, Utah.

From Salt Lake City, those of us going in the easterly direction took a train to Omaha, Nebraska. Arriving at Omaha during midafternoon, there was no train or bus service to Yankton, South Dakota, any more that day. Thus, the only alternative was hitchhiking. I found my way to US Highway 81 and started hitchhiking. Soon I was able to catch a ride with a fellow, who said he was going to Yankton. This was ideal, ---until he told me he had changed his mind and would be going west at the next "main" intersection. When we arrived at the next "main" intersection, we were south of Norfolk, Nebraska. He stopped and

I got off. It was now late afternoon and the sun was getting closer to setting. While I had hopefully been waiting for a ride to Yankton, I spotted a haystack in the nearby hayfield. At this point traffic seemed to be nil, as the US had gas rationing during this era. And it being supper hour, I decided to climb the fence and spend the night in the haystack, which I did.

With the arrival of dawn, I saw "lights" coming up US 81. I crawled out of the niche from the haystack, started for the road, climbed the fence and got to the highway before the driver in the panel arrived. He stopped. He told me he was going to Yankton and offered me a ride. I gratefully accepted.

From Yankton I was able to catch a ride to Meridian Corner, at the Junction of US18-US-81.

It was about eight AM when I arrived at Meridian Corner. Carl Anderson, who lived across the road from Edward Massey's, arrived at the intersection about the same time. He was on a tractor, on his way to do field work, on land he owned, in the same section as our (F. August) farm. He stopped and I caught a ride with him on his tractor. Arriving at his field, he stopped. I got off the tractor and walked the last mile home.

The ten-day furlough went by quickly.

Sam's Story

Figure 7: Sam home on furlough.

31

Back at camp we trained at various things until we were told we
would be transferring. This time our destination will be Ft. Lewis,
Washington state. Leaving San Diego in a vehicle convoy, we
headed north on the Coastal Highway 101. This was an enlivening
trip, as much of the scenery was of mountain and ocean view. The
convoy in which we traveled consisted of a Command Car, in
which the Captain and two lieutenants ride, a survey vehicle, four
gun trucks, four ammunition trucks, a kitchen truck, two signal
sections vehicles, a weapon's carrier, a jeep, and a supply truck.

Gun mover of 222 field artillery

Figure 8: Gun mover of 222 Field Artillery.

Figure 9: JC (James) Callis filling gas in a gun mover. JC and Sam picked up a couple in Czechoslovakia who were to be witnesses at the Nuremberg Trials in Germany.

The convoy, in which we traveled, consisted of four batteries. A Battery, B Battery, and C Battery and Headquarters' Battery. En route to Ft Lewis, we spent one night in a forest in Oregon. Bedding down for the night, some of the GIs had an air mattress for their sleeping bag. During the night, while sleeping, quite a heavy rainstorm developed. In the morning, when the guys started awakening, those with the air mattress found they'd floated some distance from where they'd bedded down. They didn't even get soaked. Myself, I slept in a pup tent.

After breakfast, and getting organized, we continued on to Ft. Lewis, near Olympia and Tacoma, Washington. Here our unit trained in Field Artillery and Physical Training. We were soon able to march, with full pack, for twenty-six miles in six hours. From the barracks at Ft. Lewis, we were able to see the gates of the Army Cavalry grounds. The slogan that adorned the gate to the opening of the cavalry grounds, read: "THROUGH THESE GATES PASS THE MOST BEAUTIFUL ASSES IN THE WORLD".!! And they were. At times we were able to witness the cavalry put their horses and mules through their paces. It was quite a sight to see the mules, and horses with their backpacks maneuver in the mountains, as part of their training.

Figure 10: Sam at Ft. Lewis WA.

Figure 11: Barracks at Ft Lewis WA.

Figure 12: Reveille at Ft. Lewis, WA.

Figure 13: Signal section crew training maneuvers at Yakima.

Figure 14: Training maneuvers at Yakima.
Figure 15: Natches Pass on Mt. Rainier.

Several times the 204th Artillery Unit left Ft. Lewis for a large desert in the Yakima area, by way of Natches Pass, going by way of Mt. Rainier National Park. The Army used this route, weather permitting, as it was a shorter route. During the off-season, we used the main highway.

In the Yakima area, we bivouacked, while on maneuvers. During this time we practiced firing the artillery guns. On one of these expeditions, while the convoy was traveling the Natches Pass, we stopped at the very foothills of Mt. Rainier for a routine break. We GIs had a chance to spend some energy, throwing snowballs.

Figure 16: Snowball fight on Mt Rainier.

In the Yakima area there were many orchards of apples and other fruit trees. Being in the desert, there was much irrigating, with water from the Natches River. This type of farming was interesting to me, a South Dakota person, as this was before irrigating our area.

While maneuvering in the Yakima area, the officers informed us, the canneries and fruit packinghouses were short of help------and they were hiring. They told us we could apply for a job, on our

Figure 17: Young orchards at the base of Mt. Rainier.

time off, if we cared to. Some of us did. I was able to experience packing plums in cans, for canning and stacking boxes, filled with apples, in a packinghouse. While training out in the field one day, my Mother and Father came to visit me. I was surprised they found me, as the trail to the training ground was a trail without gravel. The loose dust on this trail was so very fine and about four inches deep. Thinking back about that dust, its consistency was like dry cement we buy in bags and you know what that feels like. I was given the next day off. (It happened to be Sunday) Mom and Dad came and picked me up and I was able to spend the day with them. We went sightseeing in the area. The day passed quickly. It was so nice to be with them, if only for a day.

Figure 18: Mom Martha Nusz and Sam during visit at Yakima.

After a stretch, we again were informed we'd be moving. And again we boarded a train at Ft. Lewis. We were told we were going to Tennessee. En route, it seemed we stopped at every depot, to pick up cans of cream to deliver to the next destination that had a creamery.

It was during the night, that we arrived at Edgemont, South Dakota, a very small town in the very southwestern edge of the state. The train stopped by the depot. There was no wind. The moon shown on a "soft blanket" of newly fallen snow. The snow glistened, making it appear like tiny diamonds on the ground. Viewing this scene, my eyes were drawn to a small village church, on a knoll about block or two away. This whole scene created a tranquil atmosphere that is engrained in my mind to this day.

Figure 19: Near Edgemont, SD while on train ride to Tennessee.

However, the spell was soon broken, when we were ordered to alight and get in formation to exercise. We did this for about fifteen minutes, after which we were ordered to return to the train. All too soon we had to leave this tranquil setting, but when I think about it, I envision this serene peaceful scene.

Figure 20: Picture from the train ride to Tennessee.

The last memorable stop was at Chicago, Illinois. Looking out the window on the side of the train where I was seated, all I could see was railroad track, after railroad track, after railroad track for; I 'm sure, one-fourth mile. Looking out the window on the other side, all I saw were many tall buildings of various heights. To a "country boy" from South Dakota, everyone seemed gigantic.

The train took off again and when arrived at our destination, it was Camp Forrest, Tennessee.

While the main base was Camp Forrest, we maneuvered, bivouacked, practiced mock war and trained for other details in Georgia, Kentucky, North Carolina, Tennessee and Louisiana. I no longer can recall the sequence of those activities, as they happened frequently.

Figure 21: A fellow GI insulating his tent with snow on maneuvers in Tennessee.

Having returned from some assignment, this one time, one hundred fifty of us GIs were told of an assignment coming up. We, one hundred fifty GIs, were taken by truck to a camp in western North Carolina. Sometime after we had arrived, we assembled for information and instructions.

a "break" during a convoy

Figure 22: Break time during a Convoy.

We were informed, in words to the effect of the following, "Early tomorrow you will be driving in a convoy of vehicles to Camp Polk, Louisiana. The vehicles will be trucks, weapon's carriers, and jeeps. Two drivers will be assigned to each vehicle. Each of you will receive a sack lunch for your noon lunch and a meal ticket for a "named restaurant" in Texarkana, Texas, for the evening meal. You will follow the lead vehicle, which will travel at approximately 45 to 50 MPH. The following vehicles will try to pace their speed to travel at 100-yard intervals. You will have a rest stop, approximately every one and half hour."

After a night's sleep, we arose early and had a substantial breakfast. We started out on this convoy, invigorated and full of enthusiasm. With best intentions, we tried to maintain a steady, evenly spaced drive. We ate our lunch while the other driver took his turn driving. Also I enjoyed scenery I'd never before seen. But as the day went on, the steady line we tried to maintain, became staggered and at times the driving varied from 30 to 60 MPH.

It was dark when we arrived at Texarkana for our evening meal. We entered the restaurant, ordered and ate our meal, and enjoyed the change of pace. When we had finished, we turned in our meal ticket as we left. Not everyone however must have been hungry, as some of the GIs turned their ticket in for HI Point Beer. It was time to get moving. We needed to get to an airport en route, where we were to spend the night.

It was around midnight when we arrived at this airport. I believe it was an Air Force Training Base. We were directed to a two-story barracks. The first floor filled in a hurry; therefore the rest of us went to the second floor. We were unaware that there were people sleeping here, but when the light switch was activated, we hear guys hollering, "Put of the * ^* *!! !** xx!! Can't you see we want to sleep?" We didn't get shook. We felt the Air Force guys don't go through the rigors in training as the GIs, in heavy Field Artillery encounter. We too, were tired and didn't fool around as we were looking forward to sleep on a bunk, and getting to sleep as they were.

Figure 23: Chow time during training. Notice the height of the table, it was common to stand outside for a meal rather than take time to sit.

After a short, good night's sleep, we took off for Camp Polk and arrived the same day. We soon received our orders. The orders were to do maneuvers on the desert. Maneuvers are not the most pleasant, as there are no bunks on which to sleep, and understandably, food isn't necessarily always available, rarely on schedule. But maneuvering during hot and humid weather, in a desert, is beyond description. Flies, mosquitoes and other insects are rampart.

But I must say, another GI (I can't remember his name.) and myself received a fortunate break. We were sent to Fort. Sill, Oklahoma, not knowing why.

When we arrived at Ft. Sill, we met, a so called 'Supervisor" and several other GIs who formed this group. I can no longer remember how many of us there were but it was under ten.

Ft. Sill was an OFFICER'S TRAINING CENTER Camp. Our group was assigned to the same area as that of the officer trainees, however not under the same strict regulations as the officer trainees.

Our group, meeting with the supervisor, were informed our assignment was to create, and build a Radio Remote Controlled Airplane, for the US Army. Being there were no blueprints or design, we had to design and invent our own. Construction began and at time changes were made, which meant changes on the blueprints also.

Sam's Story

We constructed the frame of the plane with 'ready rod.' With an air-cooled engine and a dry cell battery, we began this project. We made transformers and used vacuum tubes, (vacuum tubes were used before computer chips) condensers, a small antenna and other parts, to numerous to mention. The supervisor was most helpful, finding parts we needed to complete this project. Perfecting and completing this part of the project, and finding it to be successful, we began building two more. Each remote plane was equipped with a parachute. This parachute was in a compartment, with a spring-loaded cover, which was built into the frame of the plane. The next task was to cover the frame with canvas, which needed to be water and air proofed. We did this by painting it with varnish. Varnish came in various colors. We choose bright colors to make the planes visible in the sky. To finish constructing these planes, we attached a propeller and two wheels. At the back of the plane, we attached a skid, (underside of the plane) to slow the speed while landing. Being every plane had a parachute we had to learn to fold them. Our instructor was a lady. She was a civilian, who was very efficient. The parachute was used in case a plane was damaged or the engine stalled, or when the terrain was too rough to land and also if a plane got lost in the clouds. When any such occurred, the operator on the ground would push the parachute button, which would release the chute. The engine would stop at the same time. In so doing, we had the advantage of knowing where the plane was and where it was landing. To test our creation, we flew several Radio Remote Controlled Airplanes for the Anti-Aircraft gunners to improve the gunnery. We did this until Uncle Sam scrapped the project. For me this assignment was an educational experience and an amiable change from doing maneuvers on the desert. The same type system is used by the military today, however, much more updated and more sophisticated. You might compare it to the "Model T" and the car of the future. I was sorry that this was the end of this type of assignment, as it was something I truly enjoyed being involved with.

This project completed, we were given a pat on the shoulder, thanked for the job, well done. And then told, "You may return from where you came." And back to Camp Polk we returned.

Some years later we heard this patent was used in a four, engine, bomber, fully loaded with explosives and one pilot. Supposedly, Hitler had a factory in the Netherlands, where they were building an atomic bomb. The pilot was to fly within 100 miles from the plant and bail out, while the plane, guided by the remote control, was to knock out this target.)

Our next move was back to Camp Forrest.

Then came Thanksgiving Day, I awakened with a toothache and a swollen cheek, I reported to sick call. Sick call sent me to one of several small cubicles. The furnishing in this cubicle, as I remember was a dentist's chair. After I was situated, a dentist entered this cubicle and examined my mouth. He left without uttering a word.

Sam's Story

Doing self-diagnosis, by process of elimination, I concluded I had
a wisdom tooth problem. After a short time, a GI Medic entered.
He gave me a shot of Novocain, then left as stately as he entered.
When the third medic entered, he had a little punch and a small
ball peen hammer. He asked me to open my mouth, which I did.
Confidently, he set the punch on my tooth and with one good
whack, cracked the tooth. This procedure had me seeing twinkling
stars. Immediately the fourth medic arrived, with a pair of pliers.
He too asked me to open my mouth. I did. With the 'pliers', he
removed the broken parts of the tooth and doing what needed
doing, he said, " Now you may return to your outfit." I felt well
enough to go to the Mess Hall that Thanksgiving Day, but I can't
remember whether I ate anything.

Having done maneuvers in the mountains in Tennessee, this time
orders were to practice mock war in the woods of Tennessee.

Being we were in Field Artillery Unit, we had four 155 MM
artillery guns to practice with. We learned, as forward observers
(FO), the Morse Code and other codes, using telephones and radio
to relay instructions and learned to calibrate our instruments.
Usually F.O. operated in pairs, one pair to four guns.

First, the 155 MM Artillery gun needed to be positioned. The
gunners never see the target, as the guns are in the rears, usually
from four to eight miles.

Forward observers have to find a strategic point. From this point we would lay telephone wire to the guns. Radios were used to communicate when we were unable to lay telephone wires. When the forward observer spotted the target, large or small,, we would locate and calibrate the position. We would contact the fire direction team and have them put out a test round. From this round, forward observer would calibrate, right, left, or short, or long, as to the target. The fire direction team would then fine tune (calibrate in greater detail) and instruct the gunners, who would calibrate the instruments on the gun to direct their fire. If it was a small target, such as an army tank, one or two guns would maybe used. If it was a large target, such as an airport or small village, four guns would be used. However, if we felt four guns weren't enough, we would call on A and C Batteries for enforcement, which amounted to eight to twelve guns, shelling. After the echelons thought we had enough training, we were brought back to camp. The echelons found things for us to do for a while.

Toward the end of January, 1944, we were given a furlough. I always enjoyed coming back home to the farm. (Nusz place) Andy and Rumie always had a project going. And frequently someone would stop by or, leaving the place, I'd "run on" to someone, friend or relative to pass the time of day.

Then on Friday night your mom (Stella) and I decided to get married --- like tomorrow.

Sam's Story

Saturday was a busy day! We went to Yankton. We stopped at Delorzie's. She had a job at J.C. Penny's, but wasn't working that day. We then stopped at Juliet's, who was taking nurses training at Sacred Heart Hospital at the time. She too had time off that day. They went along to Vermillion, where we went to the University Hospital, for our blood tests and were able to get the results the same day. When we returned to Yankton, Stel and my sisters went shopping for a dress. (No gown for your Mom and no big wedding, just a practical Sunday dress or a "street" dress, as they were called in those days). We returned home and called the Clerk of Courts, (now days Registrar of Deeds) but he wasn't home. He was attending a basketball game out of town, as his son was playing.

Sunday afternoon we met Elmer and Amanda Grosz at the Clerk of Courts house in Menno, as they were going to be our attendants. Here we purchased the license. We then went to Grace Lutheran Parsonage, where Pastor Bischop married us.

Being Stel was teaching, she needed to go to school Monday morning. Tuesday evening, Bill Massey, a school board member came with his family, and told Stel she could have the rest of the week off. That was a nice thing. Then one evening Mom and Dad had my aunts and uncles over for a gathering. That too was nice to get to see them.

Come Saturday, it was the end of my furlough and I had to return to camp.

When us GIs returned to camp, after a bit we were ordered to do more practice and training. This was the last stretch for us in the USA.

Shortly thereafter, we boarded a train, which took us to New York, New York. Upon leaving, we didn't know where we were going, but along the way we found out.

Figure 24: Stella and Sam Nusz married January 30, 1944.

Sam's Story

PASSING TIME

While training in the desert in the state of Washington, the signal section while on a reprieve, awaiting future assignment, got conversing about snakes, as there were quite a few bull snakes and rattlesnakes in this area.

Someone mentioned that some states had a law against killing bull snakes. They are not poisonous and they kill rattlesnakes.

Discussing this, some go the idea to dig a foxhole type pit, catch a rattlesnake and bull snake, place them in the pit and watch how they acted.

Two of the crew went to catch a rattle and bull snake. They were lowered into the pit. Each snake crawled into a corner, making no effort to interact.

Someone then took a piece of wire and connected it to the telephone. He then put the wire down the pit and cranked the phone. When the wire touched the rattler, it became excited, but did not go near the bull snake. The excitement cased the rattlesnake bit itself and die.

Sam's Story

AN AMAZING EAGLE

Back in 1942 while I was in military training at Ft. Lewis, Washington, this one day while walking to the PX, I noticed this one GI scanning the sky. (I've forgotten his name, so I'll call him 'GI Joe'.) I was curious about what he seemed so intent about. I stopped and asked him, "What are you looking at?" Naturally I too looked up. He said, "An eagle." This eagle was leisurely circling the sky above us.

a G.I. with his pet eagle

Figure 25: The Amazing Eagle

Sam's Story

As we were standing and watching, more GIs were gathering. Suddenly this eagle started descending and GI Joe held out his arm. The eagle, without further action, came flying down and as it leveled off, it carefully landed on his arm.

GI Joe told us this was his pet eagle. He then proceeded telling us how this all came about. He owns acreage here in Washington, about 150 miles from this camp. It was there he raised this orphaned eaglet. When this young eagle matured to where it 'felt it could feel it's wings,' it flew off to wherever--- and would return to the acreage whenever, just to 'check' on things and again take off to wherever.

The eagle hung around about a half hour and flew off. GI Joe was ever amazed that the eagle was able to recognize him from so high up, at a strange place. And so were the rest of us. And how fortunate, someone was present to pictorially record this event.

Sam's Story

A BATH THAT DIDN'T HAPPEN

In the year of 1943, (Sam can't remember what month but thinks it could have been in August, as it was very warm) while camping at Camp Forrest in Tennessee, we were again sent out on maneuvers. This time we maneuvered in the forests and on the mountains. This assignment took place in three states: Kentucky, Tennessee and North Carolina.

After we finished the assignment, while returning to camp in Tennessee, we happened onto a river. Taking a break, our officer ordered us to wash our vehicle and take a bath in the river (I can't recall the name of the river).

We partially backed our vehicle into the river. We then removed our clothes and jumped into the river. SCHOCK!!! It was COLD as the water came from off the mountains. I got out of the water as quickly as I had entered. In seconds!!

The water was so very, ICY COLD, it felt like boiling water. It stung! – and I DIDN'T take a bath.

We hurried into our clothes, drove out unto the river bank and washed the vehicle as best we could, under those conditions.

After forming a convoy, we returned to Camp Forrest, Tennessee.

Sam's Story

VIVID MEMORY (FDR) (21 GUN SALUTE)

This one day at Camp Forrest, Tennessee, the GIs were instructed to remove all ammunition from their guns. Having done this, they were instructed to line the main road in camp, on both sides, in formation. After they were in proper formation, they were informed some event would occur. They were then instructed, "When you hear the 21 gun salute, stand at attention and remain thus until this event is past." Now they felt some General or person of great importance must be visiting the camp.

Sam happened to be standing on the left side of the road. Soon three cars came into view and passing from right to left, President Franklin D. Roosevelt was riding in the center vehicle, with it's top down, (imagine that today) sitting in the left corner of the back seat, wearing a hat and waving all the while.

Sam relates, "I was close enough, I could have reached out and touched his shoulder." Thus I felt very fortunate to have seen the President of the United States, in person.

Sam's Story

Sam's Story

ARMY TENTS

Serving in the army during WWII (1941-1945) living quarters varied. Some camps had barracks, some camps had box tents, while others were out in the open. Come inclement weather, pup tenses were used.

The tents were mad of heavy-duty water-proofed tarred canvas, called tarpaulin, hence tarp. During training there were two types of tens. There were the box tent and pup tent.

Box tents consisted of a full sized door on the front of the tent and a window in the 'back wall'. The box tents had a wooden floor. The sides of the tents were six feet high. The lower half of the box tent was constructed of wood, while the top half was open. In the center of the tent, a five inch wooden pole was placed to support the roof. The roof was made of tarp. And tarps to cover the sides were suspended from the roof tarp as needed. The tarp leaked if it was accidently bumped, while it was raining.

In upper or cooler parts of California the box tents had heaters. Heaters were stoked with wood or coal. Thus a chimney extended through the roof. Some box tents had the luxury of electricity. Box tents were equipped with bunks for four or six GIs.

Pup tents were four by seven feet in size, enough space for two GIs. A pup tent consisted of two identical parts, plus two folded stakes, which when opened extended to three feet and a sizeable rope. To set up the pup tent, we place the open stakes the length of the tents. The rope then was staked from front to back. Next the tarp was placed over the rope. To complete the setting up the tent was staked down with four to six stakes.

We used pup tents away from camps. They were used on maneuvers. We used them at the Smoky Mountains in Tennessee and in Yakima Training Area in Washington State. It was in this desert area at ties some GIs found a rattlesnake under their blanket in the pup tents.

After training in the States, come March 1944, we left for overseas. We landed in England. While training in England we used the pup tents. Come D-Day – no more box tents and no more pup tents. Sleeping quarters varied, combat GIs; come nice weather, rain or snow, sleeping quarters varied. We slept in fox holes, pits, large culverts, empty houses, basements or where ever or whatever felt secure. I never slept on a bunk or a bed until the war ended in May 1945.

Sam's Story

ONE EVENING OUT

On our time off, and not wanting to remain at camp, we took a bus
or hitch hiked to a town and just rambled.

While training at Ft. Lewis, Washington, this one evening, near
Yakima, we noticed some action, in progress, at this large building.
We decided to check this out. Approaching the building, we heard
very pleasing music coming from within. Naturally we entered.

There was this good music, some singing, people were dancing and
as this continued,
the dance floor became too crowded to dance. Being the seating
places were occupied, people just stood around; kind of spell
bound, listening to this pleasant, smooth music. There was
standing room only. The band performing this beautiful music
was, 'The Dorsey Brothers'. To this day it is our very favorite
music.

A BIT OF MILITARY HISTORY

America's first peacetime draft law was passed by congress in 1940. At that time they drafted men through 35 years of age. GI Joe was drafted at age of 35. When he had completed Basic Training, he was eligible to join The Reverses and return home, which he did.

-----Then PEARL HARBOR happened, December 7, 1941, and WWII was declared. The Reserves were recalled and as the rest of the draftees, were in for the duration. It was at this time that GI Joe became a member of our unit.

Thus it was at that time in history.

GOING OVERSEAS

In late March 1944 we were in Camp Forrest, Tennessee. It was from this place that we were taken to board a train, to where, we did not know.

Not paying any special attention while traveling, suddenly we realized we were in Canada. Now we were confused – but after several hours, we were back in the States.

On this train ride, the train stopped at times but we were not allowed to step off the train. When the train made the final stop, we were at the Deporting Camp in New York, NY. We were told the reason we had gone to Canada was to "throw" or confuse the enemy, in case they were observing.

Here in New York, we were given three days to meander, however we were only allowed out of camp in the evening.
We naturally went to see sights on Manhattan Island. We toured Grand Central Station to a degree, Yankee Stadium, and the Empire State Building. From the top of the Empire State Building we checked out New York from every angle. And we frequented the Jack Dempsey Bar, as all the soldiers were given one free drink every time they entered the bar.

Early one evening a GI by the name of Tommy Haff of Long Island invited me to his Mother's house for supper. Being on

Manhattan Island we went on the subway to their place. It was my introduction to a subway. We traveled under East River and under the Bay to get to Long Island.

At Mrs. Haff's house, we enjoyed a delicious home cooked meal. After a visit with Tommy's mother; Tommy, his sister and myself returned to Manhattan Island.

Another evening, two of our buddies invited several of us to a hotel where their wives were staying, each of whom had a child with them. We thought that was neat – and after a bit, we returned to the streets. I never did hear how those GI's were able to inform their wives about our going overseas.

When our "so-called furlough" came to an end, we proceeded to walk to the ship. En route to the dock, we passed by two famous ships, the Queen Mary and the Queen Elizabeth. They were magnificent ships.
After we were all aboard – naturally, the ship left the dock.

The Unit to which I was attached was the 204th Field Artillery, which was attached to the 3rd Army. B Battery drew guard duty. We thought, "This surely is the 'short stick'!" All the others had to remain below deck. I remember watching the Statue of Liberty disappear from view. At this point in time we hadn't been informed where we were going. After sailing for some time, the weather seemed colder and suddenly we saw icebergs. We were told we were close to Greenland and Iceland. Icebergs are scary.

Sam's Story

It was in this area when we encountered rough and choppy water. The tankers and freighters in our convoy would appear to disappear. Airplanes were strapped on to the freighter. At times it seemed we were on the tip of a 'big hill' and just that quickly felt we were in a deep valley. The waves on either side were higher than the ship.

Frequently we saw sharks. They seemed to swim in packs of three to five. It appeared they were heading toward the ship many times. When the waves were high, we'd see them propel themselves from one wave into another and yet another wave and disappear.

Guarding during treacherous weather was not comfortable. There were canopy type places on deck where you could go to seek some protection from the dangerous waves. But our clothes became wet from the ocean mist spraying over a person. When the clothes dried, they felt like metal and could stand on their own. The deck was wet and kind of dangerous. The stomach was bouncing up and down. This ship was a British ship and we were fed Limey food. Oatmeal, potatoes and meat, were main fare. The meat was questionable. We could not figure out what it was. Was it mutton? – The guys, who thought they knew of mutton, said, "No, it's not mutton." Someone from the ship's crew told us they thought it was kangaroo. Most of mine was fed to the sharks as we who were guards were fed on the deck.

I did have a change of heart by now, as to B Battery pulling the "short stick". By now the floors of lower decks were slippery from barfing and… the stench, I can't describe!

However, there were some calm days on this trip.

On a very dark night on the eleventh day, we docked. We found out that we were docked at Liverpool England.

The European Theater

LANDING AT ENGLAND: SPRING 1944

It was a very dark night in April 1944 when the troop ship we were on arrived at Liverpool, England.

In total darkness, we disembarked. We immediately prepared for a march by donning our full packs, which weighed around 85 pounds. A full pack included a mess kit, canteen, extra socks, underwear, first aid kit, blanket, gun belt, rifle and etc.

With the full pack on our back we started marching. It was dark!! There was no light of any kind while we were marching ---not even as much as a cigarette or candle could produce. There were no residents visible, if there were any out and about that night. The GI in front or beside you while marching, was the only living being we were aware of. However rubble from bombed out buildings was recognizable, at times, provided you were close by the edge of the sidewalk.   While we were marching, guards were checking for lights and any questionable action. We marched most of the night until we arrived at a large sheep pasture at the outskirts of a different town. We remained there until the following morning.

It was here that all 'Battery's,' received all new equipment, such as trucks, artillery guns, weapon's carriers, jeeps, radios, telephone

and miles and miles of telephone wire, binoculars, 50 Caliber
machine guns, ammunition and a new portable kitchen and
whatever it took to equip the kitchen, such as a gas stove, tables
and etc. Our group was Battery B.

It was while we were at this location that I was assigned,
designated driver of a ¾ ton weapon's carrier, four-wheel drive
truck, with no top, a winch, and a 50-caliber gun.
From this location, "B Battery" moved the big equipment to a very
sparsely inhabited steep, 'rolly', grassy covered area, to check out
and test our new equipment. En route we saw several
sheepherders, as this was sheep county. Having completed this
project we moved to Ludlow with all "B Battery" equipment.

"B Battery" had received a collection of 2" by 2" silhouetted
slides, of aircraft. The object was to identify enemy aircraft. Well,
it was very difficult, really impossible for a group, to study these
small slides at one time. Another GI and myself were asked to
build a projector. Items needed to build the projector were: wood,
which came from an apple box (apples, in our day were packed in
wooden boxes or bushel baskets, the kind I use for a "library", in
our upstairs, west bedroom), frosted glass, flashlight lens and a
light bulb. After the projector was completed, classes for
identifying slides of aircraft got underway. Using the projector,
while studying the silhouette slides proved to be beneficial in
recognizing the enemy aircraft, once the United States got involved
in the war.

Sam's Story

When our lieutenant, Lt. Carr had leisure time, at times he would tell me to get the weapon's carrier and ask another GI to join us for an excursion. It seems he preferred sights like churches, cathedrals, castles (outside only), and cemeteries. Visiting those cemeteries was always eventful. Some tombs dated back to the year, 1200. Cathedrals had no heating systems. The people came dressed in heavy garments. Most churches we visited had bodies of people, of some prominence, buried under the floor of the church. The tomb was covered with a marble slab, with the person's name engraved on it.

Driving in England was an experience and a challenge, as the streets were narrow and everyone drives on the left side of the roads and streets. However, there was little car and truck traffic during that era.

Heavy traffic proved to be bicycles. When coming upon the bicycle traffic, at the time the work shift changed, you drove the same speed as the bicycles, as it was solid bicycles. It was impossible to penetrate the traffic.

We belonged to "B Battery of the 204th Field Artillery Battalion. A battalion consists of five batteries. This battalion was part of the 20th Corps, which was part of Patton's 3rd Army.

"A Battery", "B Battery", "C Battery", "Service Battery", and "Headquarters Battery" are the five batteries that make up a battalion.

"A", "B", and "C" batteries are relegated gun units. There were 4---155 millimeter guns to a battery. Then there was the Service battery that supplied us with ammunition, fuel and purified water, food and other feasible essentials, when possible.

Figure 26: The "Bad News" Truck, which Sam drove while serving overseas and some of his buddies.

The fifth battery was headquarters. Headquarters managed the battalion. Managing the battalion included, informing us as to where we had come from and where we were going. They managed all personal records, computing fire missions, keeping a

Sam's Story

daily diary as to how many tanks and heavy equipment were destroyed and damaged. Likewise, they kept records of the loss of soldiers, including enemy statistics. Whenever we moved from one position to another, the headquarters battery brought a telephone line into the battery's switchboard. The Signal Section consisted of five GIs. We laid a line from the switchboard to the guns. Other lines were laid to observation points and to the Captain's headquarters.

The Battery had orders to remove all battalion and Corp's identification from all vehicles. To identify the vehicles, each vehicle had to have a name for local identification. Each name had to start with the letter of their battery. Being we were "B Battery GIs, the name needed to start with "B". A GI from service section of "B" battery came by and asked me whether it was OK with me to label the weapon's carrier truck, "BAD NUSZ". (Nusz invariably was pronounced (NEWS). I consented.) See the next page for pictures of the "Bad News."

(1998)---We have a red Dodge Dakota pick-up. Cliff Handel, an insurance agent here in Menno also drives a red Dodge Dakota. His business is next to the post office. Twice I've climbed into Cliff's Dodge Dakota by mistake when I've gone for the mail. To identify our pick-up, we placed a "BAD NUSZ" decal on the side of our pick-up – Stel.

Figure 27: The signal section with the "Bad News" Truck.

Sam's Story

LOSING MY BEE BEES

The signal section was laying telephone wires. We were laying this wire on a steep hillside. I was in the back of the truck, checking the wire.

Suddenly I was blown off the back of the truck. Evidently something close by exploded and the concussion caused me to fall off backwards. My head hit a rock and I was out of it for some time. Someone took me to the medics. I had a two to three inch gash behind my right ear. The medics took care of me for maybe an hour, just enough time to sew me up then was returned to the signal crew.

Thereafter, depending what was going on someone from the signal section crew would say, "Yep, Sam lost his bee bees."

Figure 28: The Bad News with some of the guys who depended on it and each other.

CLEAN-UP DAY

Figure 29: Clean-up day was used to clean and organize equipment.

Sometime during the time of army training I was assigned to the Signal Section. I was designated as the driver of the Weapon's Carrier, a truck, which later became labeled, BAD NUSZ. A 50-caliber machine gun was mounted on this vehicle. Also, it was loaded with communication equipment, such as telephones, miles of telephone wire, switchboard and radios.

Sam's Story

Ever so often we'd be notified, 'Today is Clean-up Day." Those
assigned to driving a vehicle were responsible for keeping the
vehicle clean. We would clean the interior and the exterior of the
equipment.

This one time when given the notice, "Clean-up Day", we were
pressed for time. I decided to get this "clean-up" job done in a
hurry, so I wouldn't get 'gigged' or disciplined. I quite liberally
dampened a rag with diesel fuel and wiped the outside with it.
This cleaned the vehicle without streaking and enhanced the color.
When the Inspection Officer came by, he stopped for a bit, looking
at the vehicle with a puzzled look. He informed us to remain as we
were.

Now I was becoming concerned I might have done the wrong thing
by wiping the truck with diesel fuel. Sometime later the Inspector
returned with more officers. They too studied this truck for some
time. After a discussion, I was given a great compliment on the
appearance of this Weapons' Carrier.

Thereafter when cleaning vehicles and equipment, they had the
whole Unit using this method, but using a different oil base liquid
for cleaning.

I understand that now yet the Army uses this method on their
equipment as it also prevents oxidation.

Figure 30: Sam cleaning up for a date. (ha ha) Their helmets had multiple purposes; one was as a washbasin.

Figure 31: Cleaning guns. The cleaning rags are hanging on the 155 mm barrel. Sam didn't clean the guns. That was the gunners responsibly. The gunners told dad they had to clean the 155 mm gun during heavy fire, so they poured a bucket of water down the barrel. The barrel was so hot the water all evaporated; nothing came out the bottom of the barrel. After cleaning they continued shooting.

CUTTING HAIR

During training 150 GIs belonged to B Battery. I was one of them.
During his time also, we occasionally were subjected to personal
'Clean –up Day'.

**Figure 32: Even in the field there was time dedicated cleaning up and
getting haircuts. Sam's job on these days was to cut hair. Sam is taking
a break, sitting in the jeep reading "The Stars & Stripes."**

Sam's Story

This one-day we were asked to raise our hand if we had had some experience cutting hair. Another GI, by name of Ellis Hatch of Utah and myself raised our hand. That day we were given a cape for covering the shoulders, a hand clipper, a scissors and a comb. Also that day we became the official Barbers of B Battery.
Some of those 'Clean –up Days', Ellis and I cut 100 head of hair. We gave those GIs nice haircuts. The big deal about this was, we received 10 cents for a haircut. Some of the Captains and Lieutenants gave us 35 cents.

All in all I enjoyed doing this and appreciated the pay.

Figure 33: First bath in over year. "It didn't even feel so good. It was cold."

Sam's Story

Sam's Story

FOXHOLES

During the time GIs took basic training in the States, before WWII began, digging a foxhole was part of the routine.

Then came Pearl Harbor and a few years later, D-Day, The Normandy Invasion. Finally the push in Germany and that gave rise to a different pace and attitude about digging a foxhole. Time involved digging foxholes varies as to the situation you are presently in, also the availability of tools and soil conditions.

During waking hours in war areas, there is much motion and commotion and a definite need for foxholes.

To dig a foxhole for sleeping: you dig a hole about the length of your body and deep enough so the GI would be out of sight of the enemy. The width is narrow, just wide enough for you to fit in quite snugly, sideways---- so if a tank passed over, a soldier wouldn't get crushed. For forward observers, it was a bit different. Usually a forward observer would try to find the highest possible point and if there was a shrub in the area, that would be a plus, to dig a foxhole. For forward observers, the foxhole needed to be larger in area and deeper as they needed it for setting up instruments to observe the enemy. This is called Observation Point or OP.

Sam's Story

Generally two GIs, forward observers worked together, if possible.
At times it was more feasible for each to have his own foxhole. In
that case, they pulled a wire between themselves to communicate.

Forward observers send information to the big Artillery gunners
who may have been stationed eight miles from the target. The
gunners never see the target.

At times telephone wires were pulled from guns to the OP. This
was done when they figured it was too dangerous to use the radios.
To break the monotony, imagine during heavy firing someone, at
times, would holler   out saying, "And some "so and so"
(***@@#) volunteered for this!!"

And can you imagine awakening in a foxhole during a rain or
snowstorm?
And can you imagine living this way for one and a half years?

A BED FEELS GOOD!!!!

Figure 34: Sam and a buddy, Walker, in a foxhole in France. The Telephone switchboard was hidden in the foxhole, which was on top of a big hill under a bush - we could see the German's but they couldn't see us.

Sam's Story

Sam's Story

INJURIES

This one time Ellis Hatch and I were digging a foxhole, Ellis using a pick and I was using a shovel. We had a good beat a going, when suddenly I got hit on the top of my head with the pick.

Being there was a gush and it was bleeding, I went to the medics. They shaved the area and sprinkled a bit of sulfur in the wound and began closing it by sewing. They did not deaden the area. The doctor said they didn't need it to because the skin on the skull has no feeling. He was right, it didn't hurt. After he was finished I returned to where I had come, in the meantime, Ellis had finished digging the foxhole.

Sam's Story

Sam's Story

3,000   PLANE RAID

A few days or so after the Normandy Invasion in 1944, things were not going so well with us GI's on the front line. At this time our (US) front line was very short. Occasionally I felt we were being pushed back into the ocean.

While I was in a foxhole, I began hearing bombers and some bombing, also the German Anti Air Craft firing. I didn't know what this sound was. The drone of the planes with the incessant bombing explosion, created a solid sound. It kept intensifying to a point I was not able to distinguish one bomb explosion form another. I do not know how long it lasted--- but it sounded like one lengthy, continual explosion. It was the weirdest sound I ever heard. I really can't describe it.

After this point I got out of the foxhole and watched what was taking place. I didn't know what was happening,

However, now the US and British bombers were returning. It was quite a sight, seeing these many planes returning to England, one by one. Some with part of a wing missing, some with part of a tail missing, or an engine out of commission and others with a variety of damage. It was as the lyric of a song, which was frequently heard during WW II, expressed, 'Coming in on A Wing and A Prayer.'

Now I realized we weren't fighting the war alone. We were now able to move forward. It was a good feeling. Sometime during this time I was told, it was a "3,000 plane raid."

Sam's Story

WHAT A NIGHT

Returning from a mission late this one afternoon, we were fed a meal. At this time we were told, we would be staying in this area, which was a hay meadow.

After we had finished our appreciated meal, we spread out in this meadow and each GI began digging a foxhole for the night.

The approximate dimension of a foxhole was 12 inches wide and 20 inches deep, wide enough for a comfortable fit, while lying on your side. This shape was designed for safety reasons in case an enemy or 'friendly' army tank passed over. A tank track is wider than 12 inches. By the time we had finished digging the foxhole, it was time to crawl in, and get some sleep.

When I awoke in the morning, I assumed a German soldier must have passed or crossed over my foxhole, as here lay a German soldier's back pack.

I noticed several GIs, a ways off in deep discussion. I joined them. It was said a German soldier had thrown a hand grenade in the crotch of a C Battery's 155 mm gun, killing several of our GIs. We concluded this soldier must have run over my foxhole, due to the evidence.

We concluded the soldier, in the process of a quick get-away, after tossing the grenade, discarded extra or all baggage or stumbled over the heap of ground, from digging the foxhole. Whatever – I had slept through the plight.

Sam's Story

A CAPTURED ENEMY SOLDIER

In Germany during WWII, this one night while I was tending the Battery B switchboard I was notified to report to headquarters.

A Native American, by name of Michelle, had brought a Nazi SS prisoner, whom he had captured, to headquarters. The officer asked me to interpret as he knew I could speak the German language.

The Nazi SS prisoner was asked to remove his shoes as not to attempt an escape. He did remove his shoes.

We began questioning him----but to no avail, he refused to talk. There was no way we could get a word out of him. Thus after, I cannot remember how long, we gave up for the time being.

With the dawning of a new day, we again attempted to question him but he never did speak. Since we had no success in questioning him, it was decided to transfer him.

At this time he was given his shoes and asked him to put on his shoes, but he refused to do that. We then made him walk, barefoot to a jeep and had him climb on the hood, holding his shoes.

Someone then drove him to The Army of Occupations, who took care of German civilians, prisoners and displaced persons.

Sam's Story

A NIGHT IN THE BLACK FOREST

One of the 155 Artillery Gun and Truck crews and part of the
Signal crew of Battery B had been stationed in the Black Forest in
Germany, when we received orders to move. The weather
conditions were miserable. It was drizzly, snowy and COLD!

The road we needed to take was a narrow, one way, dirt road
through the forest. Trees were close to the road on both sides,
leaving no room for passing.

The signal crew's, weapon's carrier did not have a cab nor
windshield, nor lights. Vehicle lights were disconnected during
the war. It had a 50 caliber machine gun mounted on it. The
operator of the machine gun and myself being the driver, were the
only occupants on the weapon's carrier.

As we started to leave, it so happened that the gun crew was ahead
of us. As time went on, suddenly the gun crew, with the 155
artillery gun got stuck. The gun crew tried to pull themselves free,
by placing a cable around one of the bigger trees, using the wench
on the truck—but the tree gave way.

I then tried to get off the weapon's carrier to see if I could help---
but to my surprise, I was frozen to the seat. With a few jerks, I
was able to get off the seat.

101

A decision was made to place the cable around two, side by side trees. They repeated the procedure. This time it was successful. Again we were on our way.

It was a long, cold night – and no hot coffee.

Sam's Story

HAVE YOU EVER BEEN, REALLY HUNGRY

A combat veteran friend related the following incident, that happened to himself and several GIs, who were surrounded by the enemy for several days.

After about so long they became really hungry. It so happened there were two Native Americans in this group. These two GIs began sneaking around the rubble. After some time, one of them returned, with a snake. He efficiently proceeded to skin the snake. He asked us whether anyone wanted to eat.

The other GI followed with a mouse. He too successfully striped the skin off the mouse. He then asked, "Anyone want to eat?" But before anyone could answer, he ate it. He said, "It was too small to share." (I do not know whether anyone would have answered, anyway.)

This meat was raw. We did not dare to start a fire for our own protection.

Eventually some American GIs liberated them.

Sam's Story

HEDGEROWS IN FRANCE

Figure 35: German prisoners.

War is war!! But when fighting in France, the GI's were confronted with an obstacle foreign to them, HEDGEROWS.

A hedgerow is a mound of dirt approximately five feet high and eight feet wide and the full length of a field.

Ever so often there was a gateway for cattle and farm equipment to pass through. Hedgerows were constructed for a windbreak, to prevent erosion and or in place of a fence. (These maybe were constructed before fences as I did not see any fences in France.)

Over the years, trees grew to fifteen feet or taller. Shrubs and underbrush grew to such a mass it was discouraging and almost impossible for a human to pass through.

Also, enemy had planted mines on the gateway. They also had machine guns set up and zeroed in on the gateway.

When a GI tried to pass through, the enemy would shoot at them and usually the GI was hit with the first shot.

When a tank tried to pass through, the mine would explode and blow the track off the tank. After a few such situations or encounters, the US Army realized, they needed to   find a method to penetrate the hedgerows. Eventually tanks were outfitted with bulldozers blades and with the help of artillery guns, blew openings into the hedgerows. Now the US Army was able to advance.

Fighting by the hedgerows was very scary, as there were times you heard the enemy on the other side of the hedgerow.

The hedgerows were one of the more scary experiences of the war.

After a battle, when things had kind of settled down, if there were any captured enemy soldiers and in some cases, soldiers who had been killed, the captured soldiers were demanded to bury their dead. After burial, a stake was positioned at the head of the grave. The soldier's helmet and dog tags were then placed on the stake.

Figure 36: German prisoners load in trucks to be taken to prison camps. This was an unusual number of German prisoners because many of them surrendered.

Figure 37: This is another view of the prisoners in figure 40.

Sam's Story

GREENS

Sometime during WW II, our unit, B-Battery of the 204th Field
Artillery was drawn from the line, to assist at the front line further
north.

En route, passing through this one French village, people were
moving along both sides of the street. Some people were placing
green branches on the street and some placed articles of clothing
on the street for us to pass over. These people were waving and
cheering us on our way for several blocks. The greens consisted
of tree and shrub branches. This was their way of expressing
appreciation for our efforts.

When I happen to think on this, I wonder whether this happened on
Palm Sunday. It could have been as during those days I'd lost
track of time much of the time.

Sam's Story

FORWARD OBSERVATION
(RUBBER GUNS)

After having spent a few days in a hospital (tent), upon being released, I thought I was being returned to the unit with which I was attached. However, I was delivered to a meadow situation where two GIs, in a jeep, met me.

They said, "Let's go!!" - ! No food, however a canteen full of water. And we were on our way to an observation point (OP), a designated area on a map provided for us.

En route to this OP, we observed what appeared to be US Artillery guns, stationed strategically, ready for action – however, doing a double take, we noticed, "These guns are weaving in the wind." What they were, were rubber guns decoys to confuse the enemy.

Duties of a forward observer are to keep under cover as much as possible and go forward to where you can observe enemy activities.

Getting close to the OP, which was quite a large barn in an open area, we parked the jeep fairly near in a ravine and camouflaged the jeep. We gathered our instruments and "snuck" off to the barn.

Scrutinizing the interior, we went for the attic. Here we commenced making holes in the roof for our instruments, to observe the fortified enemy area.

We were facing, what appeared to be a large green meadow on a hill. Observing this area, occasionally we would see a large artillery gun being hydraulically elevated, up out of the ground. After firing, the guns would recede and again be hidden, that there was no sign of anything to be seen but green meadow.

It was up to us to try to calibrate the location of these guns. This was quite a fete, as these guns did not appear simultaneously and also at a different location.

The only time we could calibrate a gun was when a gun appeared and then we'd relate "degrees" to the artillery fire station direction center, to the gunners by radio or telephone. The artillery unit was usually stationed five to eight miles in the rear of us. It took several tries for us to get the accurate location, as we could only calibrate while these guns were up and out in the open and were firing. It needed to be accurate for the GI gunners to make a direct hit on the enemy.

Jamison

Checking on a target.

Figure 38: During training Jamison is calibrating the location of the target.

A direct hit resulted in obliterating the enemy's artillery guns. This would send shrapnel and enemy personnel flying into the air!

Early one evening, one of the observers, while peeking out of a barn window in the opposite direction said, "Tonight we're going to eat!" After dark he left the premise and shortly thereafter returned with a hindquarter of beef.

In the corner of this barn was a Franklin type, four-burner stove.
We ate that night.

This barn, our observation point, we concluded must have been a
sheepherder's barn as it had an attic type area and also a small
basement space.

We stayed at this place until the city behind the hill was captured
from the backside.

After the capture, going thru this city of Metz, we saw the railroad
track system, going underground into the hill, we had been
observing. We then understood how this hill area had been
fortified.

Later we were told that before we had been assigned to this OP, a
US Infantry unit, while moving forward on this fortified enemy
area, was totally annihilated.

A TRIVIAL BIT

There are times I say to someone, "I served in the military service five years." The actual time I served was from March 22, 1941, when inducted to November 1, 1945, when I was discharged. To explain my saying this is because when war was declared, time serving, took on a different meaning.

One month actual combat is considered a month and a half for GI's. Sam served nineteen months overseas, however not all were doing actual combat. Thus, I at times, mention, "I served five years." Actual time, during combat, seemed like a long time!

Sam's Story

ANOTHER FORWARD OBSERVING EXPERIENCE
(AIRPORT)

While serving in Germany during WWII a GI by the name of Hale Jamison and myself were doing forward observing during this particular situation.

Jamison and myself happened onto a German Airport. We noticed the US Infantry was there also. We therefore assumed the Infantry had captured the Airport. However, suddenly we noticed planes with the Nazi Swastika identification on the planes and other planes with the German insignia identification on the planes, landing on this runway.

Caution set in and we made ourselves as scarce as humanly possible until we figured all the German pilots were captured. We then went on doing more forward observing.

Figure 39: Jamison standing by a German spitfire plane captured by the signal section.

Sam's Story

BREWING

This episode occurred in Germany sometime before the Battle of the Bulge.

I had returned from a forward observation assignment to where the kitchen and maintenance crew were positioned, for something to eat. While I was eating, we were catching up on happenings and such. Someone from maintenance crew was telling about an interesting find. They had found two barrels, each containing approximately 50 gallons of fermented prunes. They then inquired whether I knew anything about building a still. After a short discussion the maintenance crew was able to provide the makings necessary to build a still. An empty powder keg from an artillery gun, which was constructed of steel and lined with porcelain, plus a cover that had a vapor seal, was provided. This container had the capacity of about 10 to 15 gallons. A 20 to 30-foot piece of copper tubing was rustled up. After coiling the tube, it was attached to the cover of the container to be used as a condenser. Now they were ready for the brewing business.

They filled the "powder keg" with the fermented prunes. To heat the containers, they used a blowtorch. Controlling the heat properly, the vapor came through the container as liquid. The result: alcohol.

It so happened I had to return to forward observation again. After several days, having completed the mission, I again returned to position. I'd been looking forward to indulging in a treat of "prune liquor", but all I got was about a 3 oz. shot, they had saved for me. The rear echelons got most of it. It was pretty good stuff.

Using the same still someone had found chicken mash. Naturally they experimented with it.

The chicken mash was soaked and stilling began. Stilling is a slow process. A buddy of mine, who was tending the switch board that afternoon, asked me to take over the switchboard for a little while, while he was going to visit the guys who were stilling the mash. Either the joy juice was rather potent or he overindulged, I ended operating the switchboard all night.

Sam's Story

ANOTHER OBSERVING ASSIGNMENT
(CHURCH)

One afternoon another GI and myself were given another
assignment. The weather was cool!!

We were issued a terrain map and a radio along with our regular
equipment.

Toward evening we noticed a village within feasible distance. We
noticed the village had a church with a tall steeple.

After dark we proceeded forward, figuring this church would
provide a good observation point (OP).

Arriving in the village we aimed for the church. Arriving at the
church we entered, and made our way up the steeple.

We made a few holes in the steeple, from which we could observe
the enemy with our instruments-to send messages to the guns.

We now waited for daylight. As daylight approached we saw this
a good place for observing. We noticed bridges, enemy trucks and
enemy tanks. Observing closer in our immediate range, we saw
enemy soldiers moving in this church area.

We sent fire mission back to the Artillery for them to bomb targets we designated. This continued until the US Infantry arrived and liberated the town.

After approximately three days without provisions, we were able to come down from OP.

Naturally we headed for the kitchen truck. When we arrived, Don Brown from Kooshorem, Utah, who was one of the cooks said, "Sam, come over here and sit between the stoves. I did, as it was a warm, cozy place. Don gave me a cup of hot coffee. I don't remember what we ate, but I remember that was the best cup of coffee I drank in my life. (And to this day- 2001, still claims it.)

After this meal we proceeded to discuss another assignment.

Figure 40: The kitchen tent was a comforting sight.

Sam's Story

Figure 41: Chow line - each GI carried his own plate and utensils. Sam liberated a stainless steel teaspoon from and SS soldier which he used though his tour of duty.

Sam's Story

Figure 42: After a meal it was time to relax and discuss the future assignments.

124

Dedicated to the cooks.
The cooks were welcome sights; therefore the next two pages are dedicated to them.

Figure 43: Washing dishes-the wash kettles were put over a fire, which was built in a trench. Long tools were used to dip dishes in boiling water. Each person was responsible for his own dishes.

Figure 44: Charles Wilber also spent time in the kitchen. See page 129, "Another Enemy Observation Incident (Charles) for a memorable event Sam and Charles had together.

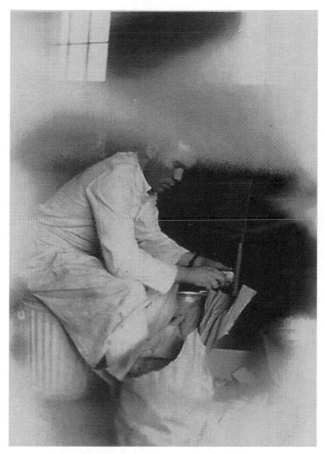

Figure 45: Don Brown peeling potatoes. Don gave Sam the best cup of coffee he has ever had.

Sam's Story

CREEK BEER

The weather was cold the time another GI and I were sent on an observing assignment. Invariably two were sent out for these assignments.

This time the observation point was on a hilltop, camouflaged from the enemy on forward position. After about two days we were thirsty.

During war there are times when fresh water is not at your beck and call.

We'd observed a creek at the foot of the hill, during our mission. At the end of the day, after evening settled into night, one of us crawled down to the creek to fill our canteens. Upon returning to OP, chlorine tablets were dropped into the canteens to disinfect the contaminated water that contained human and animal blood and waste and whatever was found in that creek.

This blend or fusion fizzed like beer. Therefore we labeled this creek water –"Creek Beer".

Sam's Story

ANOTHER ENEMY OBSERVATION INCIDENT
(CHARLES)

While my partner Charles Wilber and I were enemy observing in this small village, which had been evacuated, we happened onto this stone house. This house had been partially destroyed. It being shortly into dusk, we considered this a place to spend the night. We entered cautiously, even though the village had been evacuated didn't mean everyone had left.

While checking out this dwelling, we had spied a wood burning stove and a bucketful of eggs. We now stated a fire in the stove and fried that bucketful of eggs, the bucket being about a gallon size. Not having eaten for some time, we considered this meal to a banquet.

By now it was "dark dark" and we were tired.

We switched on the flashlight to find a place to bed down. So doing, what we saw on the kitchen wall was unreal. The wall was literally crawling with cockroaches. They came out of the cracks in the stonewalls to eat the dust on the walls for their livelihood. We lit a blowtorch and zeroed it back and forth on the walls, singeing as many cockroaches as possible.

Being tired we bedded down. Charles bedded down in a pantry type room. Three of the walls were built of stone. It was a very narrow room. I bedded in the middle of the kitchen floor and fell asleep.

As dawn approached, I awakened. Looking around I noticed much cement and stone debris on the floor.

Immediately I went to check on Charles. He was partially covered with cement and stones. I could barely see him for the debris and cement dust, but checking I could see dried blood on his face. I started pulling on his leg and hollered, "Charles, are you okay?" He hollered, "Ya!" WHAT RELIEF!!! Charles had sustained only minor injuries.

Some bombing had taken place during the night, but we'd slept thru the whole thing. Not even the cockroaches bothered us. I think they took care of us.

You can't imagine how exhausted one can get!
This is part of combat.

Just another one night stay.

Figure 46: Charles Wilber and Sam.

Sam's Story

AFTER LIBERATION

AFTER LIBERATION

After liberating Camp Dachau, the signal and forward observing section of the Artillery moved forward about one mile. This was in a small, bombed out village. Here we were setting up communications, instruments, machine guns, and etc. for the next push.

Survivors able to leave camp left in every direction. Describing these survivors I would say they were stunned, dazed, weak, half-starved, and barefooted. Wearing only black and gray striped colored clothing; some of the survivors came staggering and wobbling unto our position. Not having much time, we fed them some of our K rations. We then fitted them with a stovepipe hat and a pair of shoes, which we had found in the rubble.

Seems every house had black, stovepipe hats. These hats fascinated me. These hats were flat. Then putting your fist in it, it would pop up. Eureka! A stovepipe hat. Placing a hat on the men's head, to the best of our ability, we then instructed these men by motioning, to move in the "westerly direction" and told them to keep walking in that direction. One of the GIs instructed them in French, and I was able to do so in the German language. Army occupations then supposedly picked them up, cleaned and clothed them and provided them with medical care.

Figure 47: The back side of Camp Dachau.

These survivors were men and they made no attempt to speak or to start walking for some time. They seemed very bewildered.

Many have been the times; I've wondered about those men –
wondered – what was their status in life before Camp Dachau.
Were they political prisoners or Jews and or – what country had
been their homeland?! I've wondered, had I gotten a name or two
from them, would we have been able to communicate – or would
they even have done so.

**Figure 48: Concentration camp, Dachau. This is the same
camp, just closer and at a slightly different angle.**

Sam's Story

Sam's Story

A TERRIFIC MACHINE GUNNER

Since the war ended, at times I think of different things. I have ill feelings about some things.

I had a good friend who was a Native American. He was a good soldier and terrific machine gun operator.

During war at times you find liquor among the rubble. This friend happened on some wine this one time and indulged. Maybe because of an empty stomach it affected him rather adversely, and he went AWOL. The MP picked him up and he was placed in the guardhouse.

After the war, the US Government had some lawyers sent over to Germany to serve on war trials. Some of these were young and "cocky". The Articles of War stated, "Going AWOL during wartime, the punishment is death or any other punishment the court directs!"

After my friend's trial, he received, "Death by shooting."

I felt these young lawyers, not having seen or experienced war, thought themselves "big cheese" and didn't have much of a conscience, only a big mouth.

And that is why I don't feel so good about some things, especially this happening.

Sam's Story

Sam's Story

LIGHTING UP A TOWN

After the war, while our battery (Battery B), was stationed in this
'little town' in Germany, an officer and the service section asked
me whether it was possible to build a power plant. I said, "If we
can find a good car engine, a good car generator and a good sized
electric motor, this would be possible."

Checking through the rubble, we found the needed material. The
towns were wired, but there was no power.   In a half day we had
the little town lit up.

This was the first lighting we had seen since the war had started.

After that, the song, 'When The Lights Go On Again All Over The
World', became one of the favorites.

Copied from the magazine, 'LIVING HERE', as Marilyn Kratz
wrote it up.
Another incident, which happened just after the war while Sam
was still in Germany, was a welcome antidote to the horrors of war
and, curiously, a chance to be of service to the people who just
months before had been the "enemy."   His unit was stationed in a
small town in Germany with no electricity. An army officer asked
Sam if he could possibly build them a power plant.

"I told him if we can find a good car engine, car generator, and
good-sized electric motor, it's possible," he said. They checked

through the rubble and found the needed materials. "In half a day, we had the town lit up," Sam says. "That was the first lighting we had seen since the war started."

After that, the song, "When the Lights Go On Again All Over the World" became one of Sam's favorite war songs.

TEAMWORK

It so happened several of us came onto a train car almost full of sensitize paper for developing pictures. Fortunately one of the GI's was knowledgeable about developing pictures.

He then went to the kitchen to get ingredients to mix a solution for developing the film. He was able to come up with a formula that worked. I remember one of the items was vinegar. Sorry now at the age of 92 I can't remember what else.

He then asked me to construct a container for a magnifying glass (lens) from a broken camera, which had been salvaged from the rubble. I was able to construct and wire the container for an electric light bulb, powered by the light plant I built some time back.

Now that this GI was able to develop film, word sort of got around and when GIs found a camera, they took it and finished out the film and brought them to this GI developer. Many of the cameras had a film size that took only one inch square pictures. The GI developer was able to enlarge the pictures to various sizes. I was fortunate to work with him. And we developed many, many pictures.

Sam's Story

Sam's Story

WHITE

After WWII the unit of which I was a part, was as yet stationed in Germany.

One day a fellow GI and myself were detailed to drive to a small town in Czechoslovakia to pick up a couple.

Upon arriving in this town, we did validate where we were to pick up this couple the following day. After so doing, it was getting time to find a place for the night. We then looked up the Burgermeister (mayor) of the town. Tracking him down, we informed him of our reason for being in town. We then asked permission to spend the night in jail, as we felt the jail was the safest place to sleep. We received permission.

The following morning we fetched this couple. We believed them to be husband and wife, and delivered them to the proper authorities at Nuremberg, Germany. The woman was to testify at a trial.

The jeep we were using had space for four people. The back seat wasn't very comfortable. The road wasn't in good condition either. It was a rough ride.

After releasing the couple to the proper authority, we were assigned to a cabin some distance from Nuremberg, for a few nights.

Sam's Story

The cabins had two beds. For some reason, I can't remember it having any other furnishings. The bed had a spring and mattress. The bed was made up with white sheets, pillows with white pillowcases, plus a spread. I can't remember the color of the spread.

Having slept in pastures, weed patches, woods, and foxholes, in mud and snow at times for over a year, sleeping in a bed would truly be a welcome occasion. Well, seems I'd completely forgotten about sleeping in a bed with all its makings.

Adjusting to the bed really gave me a giddy, strange feeling. This wiggly bedspring, surrounded by the whiteness of the bedding, gave me a feeling like I was floating on a white, billowy cloud. The sensation was between traumatic and euphoria.

During wartime "white" was strictly forbidden for safety's sake. It was as taboo as having visible light at night, even striking a match out in the open.

Sam's Story

ENTERTAINMENT AFTER THE WAR

After WWII, during occupations, while yet in Germany our unit, the 204th Battalion were invited to attend some entertainment.

Anyone not on duty at the time climbed on the truck, which transported us to an open field. Here a stage of scrap lumber had been rigged up for the occasion.

Us GIs sat on the ground. There were three celebrities from the USA who put on a show of singing and dancing.

Sometime into the show, out of the clear blue, someone called for 'Sam Nusz' to appear on stage.

Almost too shy, I "forced" myself to proceed.

Arriving on stage, after some chitchat, one of the celebrities, by the name of Carol Channing, sang to me. She also gave me a hug and a kiss! Wow!!! I wish I'd remember the name of the song. Thereafter other GIs were called to the stage and received the same recognition.

After all we'd been through this was a titillating experience.

Sam's Story

Sam's Story

SOME OF THE RAVAGES OF A WAR – WWII

When fighting had ceased and WWII had ended in the European Theater, occupation began.

During wartime, as Hitler's Regime advanced, men and women, who were capable of doing any type of labor were drafted and brought to Germany, you might say as slaves to work in factories, on farms, roads, railroad, bridges, or whatever there was that needed help.   These people were from France, Russia, Italy, Austria, Poland, Czechoslovakia, and other countries "The Hitler Regime" had overtaken.

As I remember, after the war years, it seems about six of us from the 204th Battery B Artillery Unit were assigned to a rather bleak, crude camp of numerous barracks. This camp was where displaced DPs (displaced persons), from the ravages of Hitler's Regime were brought or found their way to await the time to return to their homeland.

After the war, these people arrived at this (and other camps in other areas) in spent conditions. None were overweight. However their attitude was friendly and quite jolly as we figured they had something positive to look forward to in the foreseeable future – returning to their homeland.

This camp consisted of barracks that were reconditioned for an administrative office, hospital, kitchen, and dining area and also sleeping quarters, which left much to be desired. The bunks were very crudely built from old lumber. Thin mats were used as mattresses. A bathhouse, which contained showers, laundry tubs, and a relief station were available for DP's. Our orders were to direct and guide the DP's in camp. Also, we were responsible for maintaining tranquility on the grounds. This wasn't a simple matter at times, because of the different languages.

Figure 49: This was a wonderful lady, she knew eight languages, which allowed her to communicate with a lot of people and help them get aid and find their ways home. She was a rather tall lady as Del is an average size guy.

Figure 50: This was a Lithuanian nurse at the mission.

Processing the people began as they arrived at Camp. Delousing the people was immediate. This was done by sprinkling a generous amount of disinfectant around the neck of their upper garments, and in the front and back of their shapeless trousers. After delousing, they all looked gray. DDT was used for this process.

Registration was next in line. It was vital to find out the nationality of these people. The one interpreter, on staff could speak eight languages. See Figure 52.

After registration those with health problems were sent to the hospital, which was on the grounds. As I recall, only nurses maintained this mission. I do not remember ever seeing or hearing about a doctor participating.

Figure 51: After leaving the concentration camps they were processed this is one of the German nurses at the mission who helped people after registering and Del.

Sam's Story

A GI was constantly posted in the enclosed entrance of the hospital to check the legitimacy of the people entering or leaving the building: DP's not needing health care were directed to the barracks designated as to their nationality.   Other than exercising and going to the dining hall, they remained mostly in their barracks awaiting orders to be returned to their homeland.

When there were enough people from a particular direction to fill a truck or several train boxcars, they were released and taken to their homeland.

GI's were allowed to employ some of these DP's. I especially remember three or four young men from Turkey who helped with janitor or laundry jobs, KP or whatever they could help with. These young men were good workers. They were willing, jolly, friendly, and eager to please us.   It was a sad day, the day these men received their release to return to their county. They seemed so disappointed and discouraged. I had the feeling they "hoped" they'd be able to go with us to "The States".

One day a fellow GI by the name of Herman Heitman and myself were detailed to travel with a train of about 15 carloads of DP's from Russia back to Russia. Seems Russia had more DP's than any other country. This train stopped in a very rural area approximately every one and a half hours for the people to disembark and relief themselves, women on one side of the boxcars and men on the other side. Then off again for the destination.

**Figure 52: Boxcars used to give the people rides home after
leaving the displaced persons camp.**

When we arrived at our designated station in Russia, the boxcars
were unhooked at a switch station. There were people there to take
over. At this time Heitman and myself joined the engineer in the
locomotive, to return to 'CAMP' on the hastily and temporary
repaired railroad. The return trip was ONE rugged ride.

Sam's Story

As for us GIs we did not eat at the DP Camps. An Army kitchen
had been set up, in a truck, which was parked about a 5-minute
drive from the DP Camp. When it was our turn to eat, we'd take
either a "VW" or a V8-60 Ford, which had been built in Germany
and used during the war by the Germans, to drive to the kitchen
and also for return to Camp for the next shift to use.

Our sleeping quarters were in a stripped out bus, and replaced with
bunks. This vehicle was used for sleeping only. This bus was
stationed next to the temporary hospital.

After our assignment at this camp was completed, we were sent to
another location for more "Occupation" until the project was
completed.
Because of the upheaval of WW II, some displaced persons knew
nothing about their family, whether they were alive or their
whereabouts. And also, some of these countries had been ruled
out. Those who could not be classified were as, "A man without a
country." Eventually these were given a chance to come to the
USA.

Sam's Story

A SENTIMENTAL JOURNEY HOME

After WWII ended J.C. Callis, a soldier buddy and I were assigned to contact all mayors (Buergermeisters) of a specific area in Germany. Visiting with the mayors, we presented them with typed instructions in the German and English language. We informed them what needed to be done with the displaced people from other countries, plus other information. Most every town in the War Zone had displaced people. Being able to speak some German was somewhat helpful. However, their German language was of a "higher" quality - High German.

Contemplating this assignment, we were delegated to a displaced people's camp in this area of the War Zone. Here people were segregated as to the country from whence they had come. Some of the countries were France, Austria, Holland, Norway, Sweden, Turkey, Russia, Czechoslovakia, and etc.

Army occupations completed, we were sent to Lucky Strike Camp in France to await orders to return to the USA. We remained here for approximately two weeks. During this time, our only order was, "Do not leave the Camp under any circumstances." We could do as we pleased with this time on our hands!!! We didn't even have to play ball!! Entertainment was provided. There was a library with a variety of reading material. I read, "Gone with the Wind" during this respite.

Also, a huge tent had been set up for a movie theater, in which we could watch movies. A different movie played each day and it was rerun all day, and into the late night. It was truly a relaxing time after months of being on alert.

Then came the day in October 1945 at 7 o'clock in the morning. We were ordered to get dressed. We then boarded open semi-trucks, with a rack approximately four feet high. There was no seating place, therefore we stood, lining the perimeter of the truck box and filling it with GIs.

On this beautiful cool, sunny autumn morning, all the trucks formed a convoy carrying only combat soldiers.

It was on this rolling, serpentine like, hillside road that we headed for the ship's dock.
While winding back and forth around these gently knolls, this tranquil morning, the soldiers broke into song. We could hear the GIs in other trucks singing, "Sentimental Journey Home."

Arriving at the dock approximately, 23,000 GIs boarded the troop ship, christened, "The America". I may be wrong on the number of GIs but that number always pops into my mind.

After 60 years, I continue to be "moved" when I hear the song, "Sentimental Journey Home." I then again visualize and relive the scene of 'way back when.'

Sam's Story

RETURING   HOME

Returning home after more than four and a half years in the
service, I was confronted with many different sets of
circumstances.   Having grown up on a farm with only an eighth
grade education, I pondered, "What am I going to do?"

Being REA had come into being; I was able to obtain a permit to
do electrical work. And after some time I was able to purchase a
farm. However after 'The War', the Black Market proved to be a
hindrance in purchasing machinery and equipment for farming.
This also proved to be a problem when I wanted to purchase a car.
It wasn't until February 1949, that I was able to buy my first car
from a dealer and not pay Black Market price. Up to that time we
drove a repaired, damaged pick-up. I felt I'd been denied that
time, getting on with my life.

(I was twenty nine and a half years old when I owned my first car.)

Sam's Story

REFLECTING BACK

RETURNING TO THE USA

2005   The Iraq Era

Listening and watching the news on TV these days, occasionally we see soldiers returning from serving in Iraq, relatives and friends are at the airports waiting to welcome them. The news media interviews as many of them as possible before the soldiers can escape this attention.   After leaving the airport, returning to the hometown, some are greeted with a parade.

Watching this scene, at times my mind goes back to when we were on the ship returning from WW II. After a few days we saw the Statute of Liberty in the far distance.
One of the GIs casually remarked, "Maybe when we dock, there'll be a band playing to
welcome us back."

Well, when we docked, looking down from the ship, what we saw was a gran'ma, with a little girl, standing by her side at the pier, waving. She waved for about a half hour, welcoming us.

What a contrast from today. This was before TV.

Sam's Story

Sam's Story

THINKING BACK TO THE NORMANDY INVASION

After about three years of training in different camps in the USA, our group left from New York and landed in England. Here we practiced the thing we had trained for until we left for the unknown, which turned out to be Normandy.

As I remember, it was a very foggy morning when the 204th Battalion of the 20th Corps, of which I was a part, left with a convoy from England to Normandy, France, by way of the English Channel. (I didn't know where we were going).

Along the way, the boat we were on, got hung up on a sandbar. I can't recall how long we were beached on the sandbar, but it seemed like it may have been overnight. During this time we didn't see any other boats. However, we did see several submarine periscopes going by. Not knowing whether they were friend or foe was an eerie feeling.

When a high enough tide came along, we were able to sail again. By the time we landed in Normandy, the attack had already begun. From then on there was plenty of action. Most of the time I didn't know what day of the week, or at times, what month of the year it was.

War is following orders! GIs do as they are ordered to do. Much is the unknown. And so it was when the 204th Battalion Unit was ordered to assist in liberating

Camp Dachau. Until this point in time, this type of camp was just rumor to us. What we saw was reality! What we saw was appalling! There were bodies stacked up in heaps. Other bodies were lying in rows.

Mingling with working prisoners, they revealed the bodies were those of political prisoners and Jews. These died of starvation. Many died in gas chambers. Also these bodies had been processed for the lime pits, meaning clothes and jewelry had been removed from their bodies. Gold was removed from their teeth, had also been salvaged. Supposedly the Germans had run out of fuel to fire the crematories, thus the lime pits.

A working prisoner also revealed, they were fed one-fourth pound of meat a week, consequently dying of malnutrition. The workers met the same fate.

The 204th Battalion was a unit of the 20th Corps. They received the following recognition: GHOST CORPS

The march of the 20th corps from St. Jaques to Verdun, France, 600 miles in 30 days, was one of the fastest sustained marches in history.

Sam's Story

ARMY REVEALS "GHOST CORPS" SAGA

The mysterious column that sped across nations was Waker's 20th Corps. On September 30th, 1945, the secrecy, which for weeks had surrounded the mysterious "Ghost Corps", was lifted. This disclosed major General Walton H. Wakers's 20th Corps as the spearhead of lieutenant General Patton's 3rd Army. This great eastward drive across France, demonstrated bold tactics of encirclement, which won Prime Minister Churchill's praise in parliament.

Within fifteen days. General Waker led this Corps across six rivers, namely the Sain, Seine, Verle, Morne, Aisne, and the Meure to liberate scores of town and cities including Chartres, Melun, Monterau, Fatainblur, Chareauthierry, Epernay, Peimes, and Verdun. The Corps speed was such that it thrust through the Argonne Forest in a matter of hours as compared with the several months required to take these wood in World War I. At one place the armored columns of the 20th corps knifed through the enemy defenses with such force and speed, the staff officers of a German headquarters scrambled out of their mess hall and joined the fleeing troops to avoid capture. Their food was still hot when the Americans moved in.

Incessantly pushing the Germans back and off balance, the 20th Corps captured or destroyed 200 enemy tanks, 35 personnel carriers, 500 guns of large caliber, 80 planes, and 90 vehicles. Enemy troops killed or captured exceeded 20,000.

165

Sam's Story

We were in the corps from the time we landed during Normandy invasion until the end of the war.

After go, go, go, sometimes day and night, for some months during WWII, suddenly it was over, and we began to think about returning to the USA. But before returning, the GI helped wherever needed. One of the duties was to deliver orders from Army Headquarters to the mayors in the towns of Germany.

Having completed the duty, we assisted with displaced persons. This duty completed, it was now time for our unit Battery B to turn in all equipment, such as guns, trucks, ammunition, and such.

Having done this, our army duties were terminated. Now we had time to think about returning to civilian live back in the United States. What do we have to look forward to?

It was now that us GI's were informed we needed deprogramming before our return. In essence, the following is more or less what we were told during deprogramming: " Some of you GIs are not fit to return to live among the civilians. Some of you have trained for five years to be mean and ugly; to do as you were commanded, to do it right – with no mistakes so you and your partner wouldn't get knocked out of existence. When you get back to the USA to live with civilians, it will be different. The civilians have ample money. You will have very little as your army pay is very little. The civilians own every square inch of land, so where are you going to live? You can't live in a ditch or in weed patch, as they will tell you this is our property and we don't want you on it."

"So that makes you think, think, think – do you really want to live as a civilian, no place to live, no ration stamps, no car readily available, except for black market?"
These were some of the thoughts we dealt with before our "Sentimental Journey Home"
I hope all those years weren't in vain!

(August 14, 1995 marked the 50th anniversary of the end of World War Two, the Herald welcomes any experiences servicemen wish to share with readers.)

2006---I was inducted into the military service March 22, 1941 and was discharged November 1, 1945. This amounted to 4 years and 8 months. However in wartime, while serving overseas, in actual combat, time takes on a different meaning. One year is considered one and a half years. Our Unit spent 20 calendar months overseas. Therefore the time I spent in the service was considered over five years.

Some nights seemed like a week

Sam's Story

Sam's Story

DECEMBER 7, 1941 – SIXTY YEARS AGO!

Those of you who experienced December 7, 1941—What do you recall of that day?

Sam A. Nusz remembers…(2001)

During December 1941 I was serving with an Anit-tank Unit in the US Army. We were training on a desert area in California, called "Hundred Legged".

One day a command car arrived on the scene. A fellow GI, Charles Wilbur and I were designated to report to the command car, which we did and the order we received was to return to camp with the driver of the command car.

When we arrived at Fort Ord, Charles and I were assigned to the Heavy Field Artillery Unit, which was ready to take off for San Francisco, California.

At San Francisco, we were taken to a dock where we boarded a ship. This ship soon left the harbor. Our destination was "Plumb", which was a code term for "destination unknown".

As I remember we were sailing a day or so when the ship made "about face" and we returned to the harbor. We were informed, "Destination No More".

Sam's Story

We were then told that we had been on our way to Hawaii, but the Japanese had attacked Pearl Harbor on December 7, that fateful day in history, and we were no longer needed for the assignment. This turn of events caused an unexpected situation. We were instructed to dismount and stay by the shore of the Golden Gate Bridge area until further orders. There was no place to house or feed us. The final command was, DO NOT LEAVE THIS AREA!! We meandered around the area, just to pass time. I remember sleeping under the Golden Gate Bridge one night.

The next day we were given temporary shelter in a warehouse, and at the end of the day, were fed.

SOMETIME LATER…
We were told the Japanese had fired shells at some places on the West Coast, and that this was part of their plan to invade the United States. And that the Japanese had heard – that every household in the United States had one or two guns in their houses. And this thought was enough for them to scrap the idea and put invading on hold. Fortunately it didn't happen.

Later, because of possible terrorism we were sent to guard airports and water reservoir along the west coast.

Sam's Story

D-DAY --- JUNE 1944 --- SIXTY YEARS AGO

As I remember, it was a very foggy morning when B-Battery of the 204th Artillery Battalion of the 20th Corps left England, in a ship, in a convoy for Normandy, France beachhead by way of the English Channel. At that time I didn't know where we were going.

The ship was loaded with B-Battery equipment, such as trucks, 155 caliber Howitzer, guns, ammunition, radios, telephones, miles and miles of telephone wire, the kitchen truck and whatever else that was needed.

After sailing a ways, the ship became beached on a sandbar. I can't recall how long we were hung up on the sandbar, but it was overnight, plus. During this time we didn't see any ships, but we did see several submarine periscopes going by. Not knowing whether they were friend or foe was a bit unnerving. When high tide came along, the ship was able to sail again.

When the ship approached Utah Beach, the ship went as far as was feasible. Immediately
a landing craft (LCVP) pulled alongside the ship. A crane was used to unload the ship.

When it was the turn of the weapon's carrier truck to be removed, the crane picked up the weapon's carrier with it's equipment, including a 50 caliber Howitzer gun, which was mounted on top of the truck, and the signal section crew. This vehicle was then hoisted over and above the landing craft. We were then lowered unto the landing craft.

The weapon's carrier was equipped with an overhead intake and exhaust. The fan belt had been removed. The ignition system had been totally covered with heavy grease (monkey shit) in case we had to drive in water.

The landing craft took us as close to Utah Beach as possible. The gate of the landing craft was opened and I, being driver of the weapon's carrier, drove off the craft, unto the beach. Here we joined the fireworks!!!

SERVICE RECORD

On March 22nd, 1941 twenty eight young men left Tripp, South Dakota for Sioux Falls to be inducted into the military service, namely the Army. Sam A. Nusz was one of those young men. They were the first group drafted for one year, from Hutchinson County. When Pearl Harbor was attacked, that ended the one year stint. Now it was, "For the duration."

Sam trained in seven different camps, namely, Camp Roberts and San Luis Obispo, California; Camp Ft. Lewis, Washington; Camp Forrest, Tennessee; Camp Gordon, Georgia; Camp Polk, Louisiana, and Ft. Sill, Oklahoma.

While at Camp Polk another GI and Sam received an order to be sent to Ft. Sill, not knowing why. When they arrived at Ft. Sill, they met three other GIs from different camps. After introductions they were then informed why they were called to this place. This crew of five, one of whom was the supervisor, was to develop a remote control to fly airplanes. In about two months they developed a remote and flew three planes using the remote control.

After the project was completed, they we were given a pat on the back and told; "Now you go back to where you came from." Believe it or not, we were all PFC soldiers.

Come March 22nd, 1944, the 204th Field Artillery, of the 20th Corps, of the 3rd Army was shipped to England. There they trained until they were sent to Utah Beach, Normandy. Among many battles and other actions, they were involved in the Battle of the Bulge and assisting with liberating of Camp Dachau. Sam was a forward observer in the signal section. They were combat soldiers almost for a year.

After the war, Sam was placed in a camp to help process and return displaced people to their home country.

Sam was honorably discharged November 1st, 1945.

Before the war ended we were told, the remote control patent was used in a four engine bomber. The bomber was filled with as much explosives as it could carry. One pilot manned this plane and directed it to the place in the Netherlands where 'Hitler' was supposedly, developing an atomic bomb. One hundred miles from the target, the pilot baled our and the plane was directed on the target, using the remote control. This was all the data we received.

During WWII there wasn't the modern, sophisticated, technology and scrutiny of today and of course this was before TV. Seems secrecy was more respected or contained in that era, than today.

Sam's Story

THOUGHTS OF A FIGHTING SOLDIER

After working and fighting for days and days, a soldier must take
time off for a bit of rest. So you crawl into a foxhole, nestle in and
wonder, 'How would the Lord accept a dirty, stinky GI, who
hasn't had a bath for months and months, in muddy filthy, torn and
worn out clothes?'---if-----until you doze off-------

Sam's Story

PICTURE GALLERY

The next pages are a few of Sam's pictorial memories.

**Figure 53: Bill Harris blowing revelry to
wake the soldiers for training maneuvers.**

Figure 54:

Figure 55: Solders entertaining each other.

Figure 56:

Figure 57:

Figure 58

Figure 59:

155 Artillery Gun

Figure 60:

Figure 61: Moving through France.

Figure 62: A farmer moving hay in France.

Figure 63: 1944 – A "honey wagon" liquid manure in France.

1944
"Honey wagon" in France

Figure 64: The crew taking a break while laying wire that was critical for communications. Ellis Del, George Cassel, Hugh Mickelson, ____Larson, and James Dak.

Note: The signal section crew all survived with the grace of God.

Figure 65: Sam recalls, General Patton standing at the pontoon bridge built to cross the Rhine River shouting orders to move faster.

Figure 66: Pontoon bridge crossing the Rhine River.

a pontoon bridge

Crossing the Rhine in Germany W.W.II

Figure 67: Sam added a note, LOVE SAM, while developing the picture to the family back home.

Figure 68:   The signal crew with the Bad Nusz Truck.

Figure 69: Red Cross bus handing our cookies and coffee. They only found us once as it was difficult to find us during war.

Figure 70: A letter Sam received from his mother, Martha Nusz. The soldiers name was removed/tore out sometime before he received the letter. Stella does not understand how the soldiers received their letters.

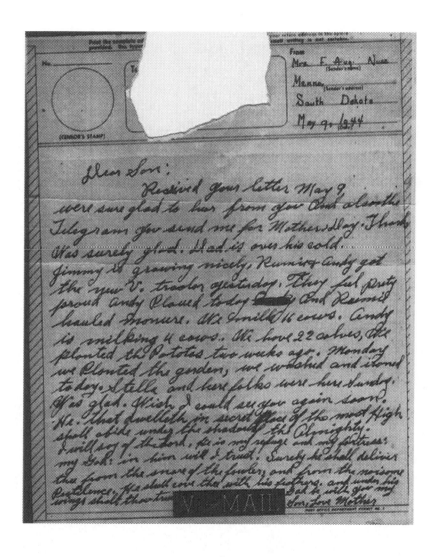

Figure 71:

Figure 72: The logo being worked on prior to the end of the war.

Sam's Story

Figure 73: Roll call after the war.

AMONG MY SOUVENIRS

At the Menno Heritage Museum are several souvenirs I mailed or brought back from the European Theater after WW II. Among them is a special sward, the kind warn by Adolph Hitler and his echelons. Watching war shows on TV echelons can be seen wearing them and it looks very professional and impressive.

This sward has the regalia which make a statement that it is a special sward. It has the swastika and silver braid on it. This sward was taken from a captured Nazi officer.

Figure 74: WWII souvenirs.

Sam in front of Hitler's Birthplace, Austria

Figure 75

Figure 76: Hitler's summer home. Ray McNeilson is wearing Hitler's black cowboy hat.

REVELATIONS OF CAMP DACHAU

The 204th Battalion of which I was a part, assisted in liberating Dachau Concentration Camp in Germany.

While liberating this camp, some of the working prisoners revealed that the bodies were those of political prisoners and Jews. These died of starvation or in gas chambers. Also these bodies had been processed for the lime pits, meaning their clothes, jewelry and the gold was removed from their teeth had been salvaged. Supposedly the Germans had run out of fuel to fire the crematories, thus the lime pits.

A working prisoner also revealed, they were fed ¼ pound of meat a week, consequently dying of malnutrition. The workers bodies were disposed in like manner.

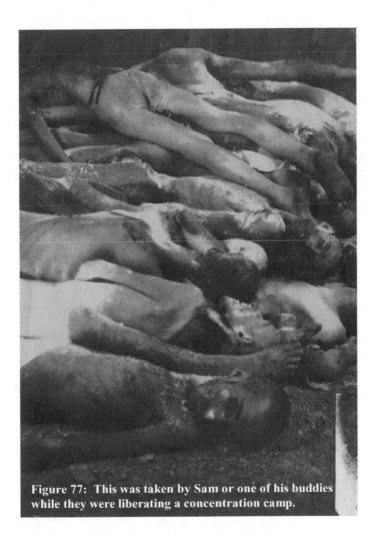

Figure 77: This was taken by Sam or one of his buddies while they were liberating a concentration camp.

Sam's Story

Sam realizes some of the pictures and events relayed are not the most pleasant but feels it is important people to understand what occurred during WWII. His generation helped to protect our country now it is up younger American citizens to prevent our government from usurping individual rights to create a government that can take away individual freedoms.

First They Came for the Jews
Pastor Martin Niemoller 1945

In Germany they first came for the Communists,
and I didn't speak up because I wasn't a Communist.

Then they came for the Jews,
and I didn't speak up because I wasn't a Jew.

Then they came for the trade unionists,
and I didn't speak up because I wasn't a trade unionist.

Then they came for the Catholics,
and I didn't speak up because I was a Protestant.

Then they came for me —
and by that time no one was left to speak up.

Niemoller, M., First they came for the jews. Retrieved from
http://www.serendipity.li/cda/niemoll.html